THE LIBRARY'S GUIDE TO
Sexual & Reproductive
HEALTH INFORMATION

BARBARA A. ALVAREZ

Editions
CHICAGO | 2023

BARBARA A. ALVAREZ is an instructor in library and information science. As a PhD student in information science, Barbara's research focus is information behavior and reproductive health information. Barbara has worked in libraries in Illinois and Wisconsin, where she developed library-community collaborations. Barbara's first book, *Embedded Business Librarianship for the Public Librarian*, was published by ALA Editions in 2016. She is a 2022 Library Journal Mover & Shaker award recipient and a 2011 American Library Association Spectrum Scholar.

© 2023 by Barbara A. Alvarez

Extensive effort has gone into ensuring the reliability of the information in this book; however, the publisher makes no warranty, express or implied, with respect to the material contained herein.

ISBN: 978-0-8389-3865-2 (paper)

Library of Congress Cataloging-in-Publication Data

Names: Alvarez, Barbara, 1989– author.
Title: The library's guide to sexual and reproductive health information / Barbara A. Alvarez.
Description: Chicago : ALA Editions, 2023. | Includes bibliographical references and index. | Summary: "This practical, user-friendly manual will demystify the process of providing sexual and reproductive health information to patrons and will provide strategies for building fact-friendly reference and program services around these topics"—Provided by publisher.
Identifiers: LCCN 2022051831 | ISBN 9780838938652 (paperback)
Subjects: LCSH: Libraries and public health. | Sexual health. | Reproductive health.
Classification: LCC Z716.42 .A46 2023 | DDC 021.2/8—dc23/eng/20221212
LC record available at https://lccn.loc.gov/2022051831

Cover design by Kimberly Hudgins. Cover image ©Alina.Alina/Adobe Stock.

Composition by Alejandra Diaz in the Source Serif Pro, Source Sans Pro and Yorkten Slab typefaces.

♾ This paper meets the requirements of ANSI/NISO Z39.48-1992 (Permanence of Paper).

Printed in the United States of America
27 26 25 24 23   5 4 3 2 1

The Library's Guide to
Sexual and Reproductive
Health Information

ALA Editions purchases fund advocacy, awareness, and accreditation programs for library professionals worldwide.

To the sexual and reproductive health advocates of the past, present, and future—*thank you*.

CONTENTS

Preface **ix**

Acknowledgments **xv**

PART I: FOUNDATION

CHAPTER ONE
Introduction to Sexual and Reproductive Health / **3**

CHAPTER TWO
Sexual and Reproductive Health Information as a Library Service / **13**

CHAPTER THREE
Sexuality / **19**

PART II: EDUCATION

CHAPTER FOUR
Sexual Health / **31**

CHAPTER FIVE
Reproductive Health / **49**

CHAPTER SIX
LGBTQIA+ Sexual and Reproductive Health Topics / **71**

PART III: IMPLEMENTATION

CHAPTER SEVEN
Sexual and Reproductive Health at Your Library / **87**

CHAPTER EIGHT
Moving Forward / **109**

Appendix: Recommended Resources **113**

Index **121**

PREFACE

Welcome

ONE OF THE most memorable stories that a fellow librarian told me involves a teenager coming up to the reference desk and asking for a book about sex. My colleague was a bit taken aback at how nonchalantly he asked for it. Perhaps she expected him to be shy or embarrassed to ask this question of a librarian—an older woman whom he didn't know. Nevertheless, she immediately typed his query into the catalog, found a list of books about sex, turned the computer toward him, and asked, "Do any of these look like what you need?" He glanced at the screen, then jumped back, his face suddenly red, and exclaimed, "No, I said *chess*!" When I first heard this story, I had a good laugh. And while I still find it funny in the way that misunderstandings can be comical, I also find it inspiring. Asking for—and providing—sexual and reproductive health information shouldn't be squirm-worthy. It should be as natural as asking for books about chess.

A few years later, I experienced just that. One afternoon, while I was working at a different public library in a different state, a young woman came right up to me at the reference desk and, in a matter-of-fact manner, asked for books on sexually transmitted infections. I was rather pleased with myself because I had *just* weeded and reordered books for our sexual and reproductive health section. As such, I felt confident giving her the latest book on that topic instead of scrambling to find something relevant on the internet.

The young woman stood at the reference desk, thumbed to the section that she needed, read it, and then handed it back to me. Satisfied with what she had found, she thanked me and was on her way. I was,

Preface

and still am, inspired by her confidence, fearlessness, and determination to get her question answered. In my mind, this woman represents the ideal scenario in which patrons feel this comfortable going to their local public library to look for whatever they need—whether it is information about chess or sex.

Sexual and reproductive health is something that impacts each and every one of us. It is a common human experience that is part of all our lived experiences. And yet we are so often socialized to be ignorant or afraid of these concepts. Many of us were raised to not ask questions about sex, feel awkward explaining our sexual or reproductive needs, or feel some sense of shame about our bodies and their natural functions. This inevitably spills into our work as public librarians; providing information and services about sexual and reproductive health takes a backseat, is not considered appropriate, or is simply forgotten. Patrons don't know if they can seek out this information at the public library, fear that they will be ridiculed for doing so, or just don't know where to start. This is unfortunate and a serious information gap.

It is in that spirit that I decided to write a book that I hope will demystify the process of providing sexual and reproductive health information to our public library patrons. I use the word *demystify* very intentionally as my goal with this book is to bring awareness to these topics, explain why they are important to public libraries, and introduce you to resources and strategies for making sexual and reproductive health information an aspect of your library's services. I firmly believe that when we educate ourselves about the basics of sexual and reproductive health, we can build stronger collections, create more inclusive services, and develop more meaningful community connections and programs. This will translate to improved information access that can empower our patrons and build healthy communities.

You might be wondering who I am and what qualifies me to write this book. First and foremost, I am a fellow library professional. I have twelve years of library and information science experience and I have worked in a variety of libraries in two states. This is my second book with ALA Editions. My first book, *Embedded Business Librarianship for the Public Librarian* (2016), was all about how public librarians can build sustainable and transformative relationships in their business communities. I have used those principles to develop community partnerships beyond the business community, including spearheading a collaboration with a health department to become a dementia-friendly library and provide dementia health information and programs. Many of the principles of this book are inspired by those concepts and experiences.

Since 2019, I have been a PhD student in information science with an emphasis on reproductive health and information access. As such, I have had many opportunities to research, write, and work alongside many different public health experts, scholars, and activists who specialize in sexual and reproductive health. This has given me unique insight into how such information can be incorporated into public library work. Indeed, I have found there to be significant gaps in literature, practices, and dialogue about such topics for librarians. However, in my communication with public librarians, I have found that there is a deep interest in this subject, and that is the impetus for this book.

I am not a medical professional and do not pretend to be. Just as you do not provide health advice to patrons, this book offers no health recommendations or guidance. Rather, it serves as a reference for core sexual and reproductive health issues, provides suggestions for continued reading and education, and discusses how you can incorporate these topics into your library services. This is an introductory-level book that provides evidence-based information, as well as key resources, concepts, and ideas that you can easily implement in your library space. There is much to learn on this topic, and my hope is that this book will serve as a gateway to your continued learning and understanding.

I also want to emphasize the importance of inclusivity. It is necessary to note that sexual and reproductive health uniquely impacts people of all sexual and gender identities. Nobody should be excluded from these crucial conversations. As such, every effort has been made to make the language and presentation of this book as inclusive as possible. However, there may be instances where certain words, phrases, or concepts are used due to citations from specific studies, research, or historical documents.

Now let's move on to the structure of this book. The first chapter introduces you to the concept of sexual and reproductive health and the framework of reproductive justice. Before we start ordering books or developing programs, it is important that we are educated about the

Preface

topics surrounding sexual and reproductive health. This chapter also emphasizes the importance of providing such information and these library services and how it relates to our duties as public librarians. The second and third chapters discuss why this work is crucial for public libraries, as well as how sexual and reproductive health information is a human right and a core foundation of public librarianship.

Chapters 4 through 6 dive into specific topics related to sexual and reproductive health, including sexually transmitted infections; contraception and sterilization; pregnancy, including miscarriages, abortion, and fertility; sexuality; and LGBTQIA+ (lesbian, gay, bisexual, transgender, queer/questioning, intersex, asexual, and other sexual identities) sexual and reproductive health. Each chapter includes an overview, definitions, and key legislation and concepts relevant to the landscape in the United States. Legislation and historical concepts are included because we must ground ourselves in where we have been as a country and where we are going. Only with that knowledge can we effectively incorporate sexual and reproductive health information into our library services.

After we have a firm understanding of the different areas of sexual and reproductive health, as well as the opportunities for collection development, reference, and resources, in the final part of the book, we consider the importance of compassionate collaborative work, including educational programs, community partnerships, and advice for integrating sexual and reproductive health information into your library practice. We connect all these elements of providing library services for sexual and reproductive health information in these final two chapters. The discussion solidifies the value of such services to our communities and presents initial steps that you can take to make this a manageable and sustainable process.

The book ends with an appendix that includes a list of recommended books and online resources to incorporate into your collection as well as sources for your continued education. Note also that each chapter ends with reflection questions that are another good source of continuing education. These questions are opportunities for you to consider what you've learned and how it relates to your library and information services. Answer these on your own or in collaboration with a colleague—they will be useful either way! Additionally, you may find it helpful to use a pen or pencil when reading this book to take notes about specific concepts, topics, and themes that you can explore in more detail later on.

Last, but certainly not least, I recognize that beyond being library professionals, we are individuals who each have core personal values and experiences that may make us feel very passionately about some of the topics discussed in this book. Human beings are complex and so are our lived experiences. Please know that I do not take that lightly and have written this book with that in mind. I also congratulate you in your efforts to provide these resources to your communities.

Sexual and reproductive health information is hugely important for public libraries and their patrons. I feel confident that by the end of this book you will be equipped with the foundational knowledge, resources, and tools to start making important inroads for the health and well-being of all who seek this information. Let's get started!

ACKNOWLEDGMENTS

I WOULD LIKE to extend my sincere gratitude to the many sexual and reproductive health scholars, activists, authors, educators, and advocates whom I have had the privilege to learn from and/or work alongside. I am inspired by not only the work that you do but also your kindness and warmth. Thank you for giving me opportunities to grow as a professional, an academic, and a person.

This gratitude is extended to the activists, experts, and authors whom I have never met but from whom I have learned a great deal. I am most especially inspired by the works and writings of Helen Rodríguez Trías, Loretta J. Ross, and Jennifer Gunter. Thank you for so many important and necessary discussions and teachings.

Thank you to the countless library professionals that I have had the privilege to work alongside and the thousands of others that I have not met. I am inspired by the work that librarians do each and every day.

Thank you to my amazing editor, Jamie Santoro. I am so grateful to have worked with you for a second time. Your encouragement, advice, and insights are unparalleled. Thank you for believing in this book and helping me develop a framework.

Thank you to my husband, Nick, for your unwavering love. Your support on this book and in all of my professional and personal endeavors means the world to me. And a special thank you to Alice for your genuine enthusiasm and interest in this book—it gave me the boost that I needed to get writing!

PART I

Foundation

The first three chapters of this book introduce you to sexual and reproductive health, reproductive justice, intersectionality, and information access. These concepts are foundational to understanding and providing sexual and reproductive health information in our public libraries. This introduction also provides you with opportunities to reflect on your library's current collection and services, as well as on how you can create spaces that are inclusive and affirming.

CHAPTER ONE

Introduction to Sexual and Reproductive Health

WHEN YOU HEAR the term *sexual and reproductive health,* what comes to mind? Most people tend to think that the concept strictly refers to sex or pregnancy. And while those areas are certainly a part of it, sexual and reproductive health encompasses so much more than just those two areas. This chapter introduces us to the key concept of sexual and reproductive health.

Sexual and Reproductive Health Defined

Let's start with the basics by examining the three core definitions of *sexual and reproductive health,* commonly referred to as SRH. (Note: throughout this book, this phrase may be used interchangeably with SRH.) The following discussion reviews each of these definitions.

According to the United Nations Population Fund, *sexual and reproductive health* "implies that people are able to have a satisfying and safe sex life [and have] the capability to reproduce and the freedom to decide if, when, and how often to do so."[1] Meanwhile, the World Health Organization (WHO) describes both *sexual health* and *reproductive health* as a "state of physical, emotional, mental and social well-being in relation to sexuality; it is not merely the absence of disease, dysfunction or infirmity."[2] Furthermore, WHO states that *sexual health* must be "free of coercion, discrimination and violence" and that the sexual rights "of all persons must be respected, protected and fulfilled."[3] *Reproductive health* specifically means that individuals "have the capability to reproduce and the freedom to decide if, when and how often to do so."[4]

Part I: Foundation

Beyond these two definitions, the Guttmacher Institute, a research organization founded in 1968 that studies and advances sexual and reproductive health, introduced an expanded understanding of this term by emphasizing that SRH is based on sexual and reproductive rights. The Guttmacher Institute connects sexual and reproductive rights to the human rights of individuals, which means that everyone has the right to

- have their bodily integrity, privacy and personal autonomy respected
- freely define their own sexuality, including sexual orientation and gender identity and expression
- decide whether and when to be sexually active
- choose their sexual partners
- have safe and pleasurable sexual experiences
- decide whether, when and whom to marry
- decide whether, when and by what means to have a child or children, and how many children to have
- have access over their lifetimes to the information, resources, services and support necessary to achieve all the above, free from discrimination, coercion, exploitation and violence.[5]

These may seem like complex explanations, and they certainly are verbose. But for the purposes of this book, *sexual and reproductive health* essentially means that people have bodily autonomy, are empowered to make choices that are best for them, and are equipped with credible information, resources, and tools to make those choices. Because public libraries provide information to communities and foster intellectual freedom, providing sexual and reproductive health information fits squarely with that mission.

Sexual and Reproductive Health Topics

As we know, sexual and reproductive health isn't simply about sex or pregnancy. It includes a myriad of concepts related to the overall health and well-being of individuals. As such, SRH includes sexual orientation, gender identity, sexual expression, relationships, and pleasure. It also encompasses infections, pregnancy and pregnancy options, contraception, sterilization, sexual dysfunction, and freedom from sexual and gender-based violence.[6] Clearly this is a wide list of topics. For the purposes of this book, we will focus on the following:

- sexually transmitted infections
- contraception
- pregnancy
- fertility and infertility
- miscarriages
- sterilization
- abortion
- menstrual health
- sexuality
- LGBTQIA+ care
- sexual violence

Please refer to the recommended resources for further education.

Reproductive Justice: An Important Framework

Often when people speak about sexual and reproductive health matters in their social circles, the conversations tend to be based on "pro" or "anti"—"for" or "against." This is a very limited view because these conversations tend to bypass many of the factors that may compel an individual to make specific SRH-related decisions. Enter the framework of reproductive justice.

Reproductive justice, often referred to as RJ, is a term that was coined by Black activists, advocates, and health professionals at the 1994 International Conference on Population and Development in Cairo who were frustrated that the pro-choice movement alienated women of color by not addressing the very real issues associated with reproductive health decision making.[7] SisterSong, one of the most well-known reproductive justice organizations, explains how these individuals "recognized that the women's rights movement, led by and representing middle-class and wealthy white women, could not defend the needs" of women of color or of trans people and other marginalized women.[8] Essentially, they saw the impetus for a new framework that centered the needs of marginalized women, families, and communities. Therefore, reproductive justice is "the human right to maintain personal bodily autonomy, have children, not have children, and parent the children we have in safe and sustainable communities."[9] The RJ framework is significant because it asserts that reproductive health isn't just about sex, abortion, or contraception; it is a holistic lens of one's welfare and encompasses topics like housing, community safety, job opportunities, schools, (dis)ability, socioeconomic status, class, race, sexual orientation, and gender identity.

Reproductive justice is especially important because it recognizes that people of color and marginalized communities have long been denied the ability to exercise bodily autonomy and raise their families safely. There are many examples of this in American history, but I present here just a few of them.

Indigenous people have long been denied reproductive justice. In fact, for a century and a half, Indigenous children in the United States were taken from their tribal lands and forced to attend federally funded boarding schools where they were stripped of their Native American cultures and identities.[10] Brianna Theobald, an assistant professor of history at the University of Rochester and author of the book *Reproduction on the Reservation: Pregnancy, Childbirth, and Colonialism in the Long Twentieth Century,* estimates that 25 to 42 percent of native women of childbearing age were sterilized from the 1930s to the 1970s, many coercively or without full understanding of the procedure.[11] To date, Native Americans are still unable to receive affordable abortion care on the Indian Health Service Plan. The federally passed Hyde Amendment, which has been in effect for nearly fifty years, forbids the expenditure of federal funds on abortion services, except in rare cases.[12] (The Hyde Amendment also affects people on any form of federal health insurance, including Medicaid, and Peace Corps volunteers.)

Another example of lack full reproductive knowledge was in Puerto Rico, a commonwealth of the United States. In fact, the first birth control pill was unethically tested on Puerto Rican women to determine its safety and efficacy.[13] And between the 1930s and 1970s, one-third of Puerto Rican women were sterilized in a procedure that became so common it was colloquially known as "la operación," or "the operation." Through USAID grants, free sterilizations could be found outside of factories where many women worked. This resulted in Puerto Rican women having the highest sterilization rate in the world. Later studies found that many women opted for sterilization because of external pressures, like lack of family planning resources or poor living conditions, and 33 percent of recipients later felt some sort of regret for being sterilized.[14]

Compulsory sterilization was also been wielded against other marginalized communities in the United States for over 100 years. Compulsory sterilization laws were adopted by more than thirty-two states between 1907 and 1937. In 1927, the US Supreme Court ruled by a vote of 8 to 1 that states could forcibly sterilize "a person considered unfit to procreate" in *Buck v. Bell*. In total, roughly 70,000 people were sterilized against their will in the United States, and historically marginalized communities were disproportionately targeted.[15]

Mexican Americans were also targeted for forced sterilization in California with Latino men and women 23 and 59 percent more likely to be sterilized than non-Latinos.[16] In North Carolina, Black women were sterilized at more than three times the rate of white women and twelve times the rate of white men between 1950 and 1966.[17]

Although state sterilization laws have been repealed, there are still many instances of coerced sterilization. In 2009 a woman in West Virginia who was convicted of marijuana possession underwent sterilization as part of her probation, and in 2017 a Tennessee judge offered reduced jail sentences to people who "volunteered" to undergo sterilization.[18] In 2020 a nurse at a Georgia immigration detention center filed a whistleblower complaint regarding lack of medical care, unsafe work practices, and questionable hysterectomies performed on immigrant women.[19]

Black women in the United States have long experienced unfair medical practices. Enslaved African American women were separated from their children and families, raped by their white owners, and forced to breed with other slaves in order to produce more workers for plantations. Furthermore, James Marion Sims, known as the father of modern gynecology, conducted research on enslaved Black women without anesthesia or medical ethicists.[20] Sims used Black bodies to invent the vaginal speculum, which is still used for dilation and examination, as well as surgical techniques to repair vesicovaginal fistula. Beyond this, Black mothers were excluded from welfare programs, such as Mother's Pensions for single mothers and the Social Security Act of 1935, until the 1960s. Caseworkers "expected black women to be employed moms and not be stay-at-home moms like white women."[21]

Wage gaps, police brutality, and the prison industrial complex are all factors that continue to impact the sexual and reproductive health choices of Black women and communities. The Centers for Disease Control and Prevention (CDC) has reported significant health disparities related to pregnancy-related deaths. For example, Black, American Indian (AI), and Alaska Native (AN) women are two to three times more likely to die from pregnancy-related causes than are white women. In fact, pregnancy-related deaths per 100,000 live births for Black and AI/AN women older than thirty were four to five times as high as for white women.[22] These differences in health outcomes stem from broader social and economic inequities that disproportionately impact people of color, low-income communities, immigrants, LGBTQIA+ people, and other underserved groups. Factors can include economic stability; neighborhood and physical environment; education; food; community, safety, and social context; and the health care system.[23] As In Our Own Voice: National Black Women's Reproductive Justice Agenda explains, the reproductive justice framework is important because it "brings transformational change where every person has the economic, social, cultural and political power to make decisions about their sexuality, health, and families."[24]

Furthermore, members of the LGBTQIA+ community have long been pathologized and denied gender-affirming care and comprehensive health insurance. In 2020 the Trump administration removed nondiscrimination protections in health care and health insurance for LGBTQIA+ people.[25] In 2022 Governor Greg Abbott of Texas enacted a bill that allows the Texas Department of Family and Protective Services to investigate parents and doctors who provide gender-affirming care to trans children.[26] Legislative attacks on trans children and people continue in states across the country, and only 6.7 percent of LGBTQIA+ students report receiving sex education that includes positive representations of various sexual orientations and gender identities.[27]

I share these examples as I think it is necessary for us to ground ourselves in the historical and contemporary issues surrounding sexual and reproductive health. When we can better understand where we have come from and where we are at on this issue, we can provide more comprehensive collections and resources. I also believe that we can serve a role in the larger issue of dismantling systemic injustices by informing ourselves on these topics and providing information on them to our communities. Such efforts help destigmatize sexual and reproductive health information. They also help facilitate information access, which is crucial to making informed decisions about one's sexual and reproductive health and in empowering our communities. Public libraries have made many proclamations about promoting diversity, equity, and inclusion in their library spaces. If public libraries are to truly embody those values, they will see the need for reproductive justice material in library services and collections.

Final Thoughts

To be sure, this is a cursory glance at the very complex historical and contemporary realities related to sexual and reproductive health, but I hope that it demonstrates the importance of centering communities in the SRH information services that we provide. When we educate ourselves on these topics, we can provide credible and useful resources to those who need them. Whether you have done some preliminary work or are completely new to this topic, welcome—you're in the right spot.

Let's Review

- Sexual and reproductive health, or SRH, looks like a world where people have bodily autonomy, are empowered to make choices that are best for them, and are equipped with credible information, resources, and tools to make those choices.
- Public libraries empower communities to make decisions that are best for themselves and their families by providing them with credible information, resources, and tools.
- Reproductive justice, or RJ, a term coined by Black activists, advocates, and health professionals, asserts as a human right the ability to maintain personal bodily autonomy, to have or not children, and to parent children in safe and sustainable communities.

- Although sexual and reproductive health is a wide-ranging topic, this book focuses on sexually transmitted infections, contraception, pregnancy, fertility and infertility, miscarriages, sterilization, abortion, menstrual health, sexuality, and LGBTQIA+ care.
- Public libraries can stand up for diversity, equity, and inclusion by providing sexual and reproductive health information and services.

Reflection Questions

- Has your understanding of sexual and reproductive health information changed after reading the definitions in this chapter? Explain how.
- Had you heard of the reproductive justice framework before reading this chapter? What does reproductive justice mean to you?
- How do you think that these concepts relate to your work as a public librarian?

NOTES

1. "Sexual and Reproductive Health," United Nations Population Fund, www.unfpa.org/sexual-reproductive-health.
2. "Defining Sexual Health," World Health Organization (WHO), www.who.int/teams/sexual-and-reproductive-health-and-research/key-areas-of-work/sexual-health/defining-sexual-health.
3. "Defining Sexual Health," WHO.
4. "Reproductive Health," World Health Organization, www.who.int/westernpacific/health-topics/reproductive-health.
5. "Accelerate Progress: Sexual and Reproductive Health and Rights for All—Executive Summary," Guttmacher Institute, www.guttmacher.org/guttmacher-lancet-commission/accelerate-progress-executive-summary.
6. "Sexual Health," World Health Organization, www.who.int/health-topics/sexual-health#tab=tab_1.
7. "Reproductive Justice," In Our Own Voice: National Black Women's Reproductive Justice Agenda, https://blackrj.org/our-issues/reproductive-justice/.
8. "Reproductive Justice," SisterSong, www.sistersong.net/reproductive-justice.
9. "Reproductive Justice," SisterSong.

10. Rukmini Callimachi and Sharon Chischilly, "Lost Lives, Lost Culture: The Forgotten History of Indigenous Boarding Schools," *The New York Times,* November 17, 2021, https://www.nytimes.com/2021/07/19/us/us-canada-indigenous-boarding-residential-schools.html.
11. Beth Adams, "'Reproduction on the Reservation:' The History of Forced Sterilization of Native American Women," WXXI News, October 28, 2019, www.wxxinews.org/local-news/2019-10-28/reproduction-on-the-reservation-the-history-of-forced-sterilization-of-native-american-women.
12. Alina Salganicoff, Laurie Sobel, and Amrutha Ramaswamy, "The Hyde Amendment and Coverage for Abortion Services," KFF, March 5, 2021, www.kff.org/womens-health-policy/issue-brief/the-hyde-amendment-and-coverage-for-abortion-services/.
13. Erin Blakemore, "The First Birth Control Pill Used Puerto Rican Women as Guinea Pigs," History, updated March 11, 2019, www.history.com/news/birth-control-pill-history-puerto-rico-enovid.
14. Katherine Andrews, "The Dark History of Forced Sterilization of Latina Women," Panoramas, October 31, 2017, www.panoramas.pitt.edu/health-and-society/dark-history-forced-sterilization-latina-women.
15. "The Supreme Court Ruling That Led to 70,000 Forced Sterilizations," NPR, March 7, 2016, www.npr.org/sections/health-shots/2016/03/07/469478098/the-supreme-court-ruling-that-led-to-70-000-forced-sterilizations.
16. Nicole L. Novak and Natalie Lira, "California Once Targeted Latinas for Forced Sterilization," *Smithsonian Magazine,* March 22, 2018, www.smithsonianmag.com/history/california-targeted-latinas-forced-sterilization-180968567/.
17. Alexandra M. Stern, "Forced Sterilization Policies in the US Targeted Minorities and Those with Disabilities—and Lasted into the 21st Century," The Conversation, August 26, 2020, https://theconversation.com/forced-sterilization-policies-in-the-us-targeted-minorities-and-those-with-disabilities-and-lasted-into-the-21st-century-143144.
18. Sanjana Manjeshwar, "America's Forgotten History of Forced Sterilization," *Berkeley Political Review,* November 4, 2020, https://bpr.berkeley.edu/2020/11/04/americas-forgotten-history-of-forced-sterilization/.
19. Rachel Treisman, "Whistleblower Alleges 'Medical Neglect,' Questionable Hysterectomies of ICE Detainees," NPR, September 16, 2020, www.npr.org/2020/09/16/913398383/whistleblower-alleges-medical-neglect-questionable-hysterectomies-of-ice-detaine.

Part I: Foundation

20. Brynn Holland, "The 'Father of Modern Gynecology' Performed Shocking Experiments on Enslaved Women," History, updated December 4, 2018, www.history.com/news/the-father-of-modern-gynecology-performed-shocking-experiments-on-slaves.
21. Nina Banks, "Black Women's Labor Market History Reveals Deep-Seated Race and Gender Discrimination," *Working Economics Blog,* February 19, 2019, www.epi.org/blog/black-womens-labor-market-history-reveals-deep-seated-race-and-gender-discrimination/.
22. CDC Newsroom, "Racial and Ethnic Disparities Continue in Pregnancy-Related Deaths," CDC, last reviewed September 6, 2019, www.cdc.gov/media/releases/2019/p0905-racial-ethnic-disparities-pregnancy-deaths.html.
23. Nambi Ndugga and Samantha Artiga, "Disparities in Health and Health Care: 5 Key Questions and Answers," KFF, May 11, 2021, www.kff.org/racial-equity-and-health-policy/issue-brief/disparities-in-health-and-health-care-5-key-question-and-answers.
24. "HERStory," In Our Own Voice: National Black Women's Reproductive Justice Agenda, https://blackrj.org/about-us/herstory/.
25. Selena Simmons-Duffin, "Transgender Health Protections Reversed by Trump Administration," NPR, June 12, 2020, www.npr.org/sections/health-shots/2020/06/12/868073068/transgender-health-protections-reversed-by-trump-administration.
26. Vanessa Romo, "The ACLU Sues to Block Texas from Investigating Parents of Trans Youth," NPR, March 1, 2022, www.npr.org/2022/03/01/1083822027/aclu-lawsuit-texas-parents-trans-transgender-minor-abbott.
27. Joseph G. Kosciw et al., *The 2017 National School Climate Survey: The Experiences of Lesbian, Gay, Bisexual, Transgender, and Queer Youth in Our Nation's Schools* (New York: GLSEN, 2018).

CHAPTER TWO

Sexual and Reproductive Health Information as a Library Service

WELCOME TO THE second chapter! By now you should have a solid understanding of sexual and reproductive health, as well as the reproductive justice framework. I hope that this background gives you an idea of just how important this concept is for public libraries. In this chapter, we review how information access for sexual and reproductive health aligns with the values of public libraries.

SRH Information Access Is Core to Libraries

For public librarians, upholding information access is a crucial service. Indeed, it is a core library tenant. The American Library Association (ALA) in "Access to Library Resources and Services" states, "Core values of the library community such as equal access to information, intellectual freedom, and the objective stewardship and provision of information must be preserved and strengthened, now more than ever."[1] Providing SRH information is aligned with our role as public librarians.

Furthermore, ALA's *Library Bill of Rights* provides insight into how librarians can uphold intellectual freedom. First adopted in 1939 and most recently updated in 2019, the *Library Bill of Rights* affirms that libraries are spaces for the exchange of information and ideas and that material should not be restricted. In fact, a recent interpretation of the *Library Bill of Rights* explicitly states, "The American Library Association stringently and unequivocally maintains that libraries and librarians have an obligation to resist efforts that systematically exclude materials dealing with any subject matter, including sex, gender

Part I: Foundation

identity, or sexual orientation."[2] As we have learned, these topics are key to sexual and reproductive health information.

In addition to the *Library Bill of Rights,* the First Amendment protects people against the suppression of ideas and information and allows individuals to "speak, publish, read and view what they wish."[3] Essentially, the First Amendment defends intellectual freedom, which includes the right to receive information. And it is our duty as librarians to provide resources on a variety of topics, including those on sexual and reproductive health. I recognize that some librarians may not personally agree with certain SRH choices. However, this doesn't mean that information and resources should be diminished or denied. After all, public librarians work with people of all walks of life and backgrounds.[4] A later chapter discusses specific reference standards.

Our personal beliefs should not be the guiding force for the SRH information we have in our collection. Consequently, collection development plays a crucial role in making comprehensive SRH information accessible. For instance, ALA's *Freedom to Read Statement* dives into the importance of resisting censorship and suppression of materials.[5] This means that librarians must resist the urge to self-censor when selecting material for the library. In a recent study by Dr. Carolyn Carlson, 83.9 percent of respondents chose not to purchase a book for the public school library based on its content, which was largely sexual (70.5 percent) and LGBTQ (17.6 percent) in nature. As Dr. Carlson states, "If the library is deemed a place where students can access information to controversial topics . . . then the book collection should reflect that stance." Public libraries should be no different.[6] In fact, ALA affirms the right to sex education materials in libraries and "the right of youth to comprehensive, sex-related education, materials, programs, and referral services of the highest quality."[7]

This is especially important when considering the needs of individuals in a variety of health care situations. For instance, individuals may prefer to do their own research before or after meeting with a medical professional. This may make them feel more equipped to explain their concerns, symptoms, or goals when speaking with a provider. Public librarians can play a role in empowering their communities by providing collections with comprehensive sexual and reproductive health information.

SRH Information Access Is a Human Right

Beyond professional library values, statements, and policies, access to information about sexual and reproductive health is a fundamental human right. The Universal Declaration of Human Rights (UDHR) is a great place to start this conversation. UDHR, which was proclaimed by the United Nations General Assembly in 1948 and has been translated into over 500 languages, outlines "fundamental human rights to be universally protected."[8] The preamble in UDHR declares that this standard is a "recognition of the inherent dignity and of the equal and inalienable rights of all members of the human family [as] the foundation of freedom, justice and peace in the world."[9] The document outlines thirty articles to uphold this standard. Of particular importance to librarians is Article 19 that proclaims, "Everyone has the right to freedom of opinion and expression; this right includes freedom to hold opinions without interference and to seek, receive and impart information and ideas through any media and regardless of frontiers."[10] This means that we should not restrict people from accessing information, including SRH resources, that can help them make informed choices.

The World Health Organization (WHO) agrees. When describing sexual health, WHO explains that sexual health and well-being is dependent on "access to comprehensive, good-quality information about sex and sexuality."[11] WHO explains that sexual health is important not only for individual human dignity but also to the proper functioning of "the social and economic development of communities and countries."[12] That last statement may leave you wondering how access to SRH information could impact social and economic development of communities and countries. Let's unpack this by looking at the United Nations' Sustainable Development Goals (SDG).

SDG is a collection of seventeen goals that are designed to be a blueprint for ending poverty, reducing inequality, improving health and education, and strengthening economic growth. Its fifth goal specifically focuses on gender equality and calls for "universal access to sexual and reproductive health and reproductive rights."[13] Notably, it also demands "the use of enabling technology, in particular information and communications technology, to promote the empowerment of women."[14] Essentially, this goal is calling for not only comprehensive SRH information but also access to such information. And although SDG specifically includes "the empowerment of women," this action will improve the sexual health of all people.

This goal is essential because people die or are harmed when they do not have access to comprehensive SRH information. A report by the Guttmacher Institute explains that 81 percent of unintended pregnancies in lower-income countries occur due to not only a lack of contraception but also women's perceived risks of using contraception.[15] Many women in higher- and lower-income countries seek abortions when they are faced with an unintended pregnancy. Without access to contraception and abortion information, women die. In fact, WHO reported that 13.2 percent of maternal deaths worldwide can be attributed to unsafe abortion. To prevent deaths, WHO specifically calls for quality comprehensive abortion care, including the availability and accessibility of information.[16] The CDC explains that sexual health is a public health concern, and that information access can improve health not only for the individual but also for the collective.[17] This leads to healthier communities that are more likely to thrive both socially and economically.

Final Thoughts

I hope that you feel confident in knowing that providing sexual and reproductive health information connects with the mission of public libraries. Beyond the standards, research, and guidelines outlined in this section, providing SRH information lends itself to many opportunities for the public library to establish itself as a key community center. Long gone are the days of public libraries as merely information repositories. People use public libraries to learn, collaborate, and explore. By providing information, we can also build up community connections. We will discuss this again later, so stay tuned!

Chapter Two: Sexual and Reproductive Health Information as a Library Service

Let's Review

- Providing comprehensive, evidence-based sexual and reproductive health information is aligned with the values of librarianship. The *Library Bill of Rights,* ALA's *Freedom to Read Statement,* and the First Amendment value intellectual freedom, which includes queries related to SRH information.
- Access to sexual and reproductive health information is also a core value of human rights organizations. The CDC further explains that SRH is critical for public health.
- People may seek this information in the library before speaking with medical professionals or to better understand information given to them by their providers. Libraries can empower individuals to find comprehensive information. Providing this service leads to healthier communities.

Reflection Questions

- Do you sense or know of any resistance to providing sexual and reproductive health information at your library? How does that make you feel?
- Did you know that sexual and reproductive health is considered a human right? How does this change or reaffirm your idea of providing this information at your library?
- How do you think providing sexual and reproductive health information could impact your community?

NOTES

1. "Access to Library Resources and Services," American Library Association, updated October 1, 2021, www.ala.org/advocacy/intfreedom/access.
2. "Library Bill of Rights," American Library Association, www.ala.org/advocacy/intfreedom/librarybill.
3. "First Amendment and Censorship," American Library Association, updated October 2021, www.ala.org/advocacy/intfreedom/censorship.
4. Judith Haydel, "Libraries and Intellectual Freedom," The First Amendment Encyclopedia, 2009, www.mtsu.edu/first-amendment/article/1125/libraries-and-intellectual-freedom.

Part I: Foundation

5. "The Freedom to Read Statement," American Library Association, www.ala.org/advocacy/intfreedom/freedomreadstatement.
6. Carolyn Carlson, "The Fear of Retaliation: Proactie [sic] Censorship by Public School Librarians," *Michigan Reading Journal* 52, no. 3 (2020): article 4, https://scholarworks.gvsu.edu/mrj/vol52/iss3/4.
7. "ALA Policy Manual," B.8 Services and Responsibilities of Libraries (Old Number 52), American Library Association, https://www.ala.org/aboutala/governance/policymanual/updatedpolicymanual/section2/52libsvcsandrespon#B.8.6.2.
8. "Universal Declaration of Human Rights," United Nations (UN), www.un.org/en/about-us/universal-declaration-of-human-rights.
9. "Universal Declaration of Human Rights," UN.
10. "Universal Declaration of Human Rights," UN.
11. "Sexual Health," World Health Organization (WHO), www.who.int/health-topics/sexual-health#tab=tab_1.
12. "Sexual Health," WHO.
13. "The 17 Goals: Sustainable Development," United Nations (UN), https://sdgs.un.org/goals.
14. "The 17 Goals," UN.
15. Sneha Barot, "Sexual and Reproductive Health and Rights Are Key to Global Development: The Case for Ramping Up Investment," *Guttmacher Policy Review,* 18, no. 1 (2015), www.guttmacher.org/gpr/2015/02/sexual-and-reproductive-health-and-rights-are-key-global-development-case-ramping.
16. "Abortion," World Health Organization, November 25, 2021, www.who.int/news-room/fact-sheets/detail/abortion.
17. "Sexual Health," Centers for Disease Control and Prevention, last reviewed June 25, 2019, www.cdc.gov/sexualhealth/Default.html.

CHAPTER THREE

Sexuality

WE HAVE ALREADY made quite a bit of progress! The first two chapters dove into the core concepts of sexual and reproductive health and why this topic is extremely important for public libraries. Before we move on to specific issues related to sexual and reproductive health, it is important that we have a firm understanding of sexuality. To be sure, sexuality is an aspect of sexual and reproductive health, but for us to fully appreciate the upcoming chapters, one chapter dedicated solely to sexuality is necessary.

Similar to the upcoming chapters in part II, this one includes an overview about key concepts, as well as citations and reflection questions. One of the recommended resources used in the Sexual Orientation section of this chapter is the "PFLAG National Glossary of Terms."[1] PFLAG is the first and largest organization for LGBTQ+ people, their parents and families, and allies. Although this chapter has an abbreviated version of their definitions, please refer to PFLAG's full glossary for additional definitions.

Overview of Sexuality

Sexuality includes attitudes, values, and feelings that are influenced by our individual experiences and preferences, our family and culture, religion/spirituality, laws, professions, institutions, science, and politics.[2] As such, sexuality is something that can be affected by external factors, such as the way that we were raised or legislation. But sexuality

Part I: Foundation

is also something deeply personal that can transcend or complement external factors. Specifically, sexuality includes the following:

- awareness and acceptance of our own bodies and others' bodies
- sexual expression
- anatomy and physiology
- gender identity
- sexual orientation
- levels of attraction
- sexual health concepts
- reproductive health concepts

Because we will explore sexual and reproductive health concepts in later chapters, this chapter focuses on gender identity, sexual orientation, and sexual expression. These are necessary concepts for librarians to understand. When developing library collections and providing services, we should ensure that they are inclusive and provided with the understanding that everybody experiences and understands these concepts through a unique perspective.

Sex and Gender

Sex and *gender* are terms that are often used interchangeably, but they have distinct definitions that are important to understand. Sex refers to the different biological and physiological characteristics of people. Sometimes referred to as "sex assigned at birth" or "biological sex," *sex* is a label that describes a child at birth based on their external anatomy.[3] Gender encompasses the social norms, behaviors, and roles that are given to people based on their sex assigned at birth. Gender constructs also impact norms and expectations surrounding clothing, appearances, and behavior. These gendered characteristics can vary depending on the culture and society in which one resides.[4]

Gender Identity

Gender identity is how someone feels in relation to their gender. This may not be outwardly visible. For example, some people may feel that their gender identity aligns with the sex that they were assigned at birth. As such, if someone is assigned female at birth and identifies as a woman, they are considered cisgender.[5] Other people may have a gender identity that is different from their sex assigned at birth. So if someone is assigned female at birth but identifies as a man, they may consider themselves to be transgender. People who identify as nonbinary do not describe themselves as fitting exclusively into either male or female dichotomies. Instead, they may identify as both a man and a woman, outside of the binaries, or somewhere in the middle. As such, nonbinary folks may also identify as nonbinary *and* transgender or male or female.[6] People who reject static gender identities may describe themselves as genderqueer, gender variant, gender diverse, gender nonconforming, or androgynous.[7]

Last, we may think about gender identity resources and information as something exclusively for young people. That's short-sighted. Older people can also reconsider their identity for a variety of reasons. For instance, a lack of information and resources coupled with weak familial, societal, or cultural support are just a few examples of why someone may not have embraced or been aware of different gender identities at a younger age. Other people may simply come into their identities later in life—there is no one-size-fits-all time line. Therefore, we shouldn't build collections for only young people. This information is truly ageless.

GENDER INCLUSIVITY AT THE PUBLIC LIBRARY

To communicate that the public library is a place where people are accepted for who they are, consider implementing these gender-inclusive practices:

- Let staff wear buttons with their pronouns or add pronouns to name tags.
- Include pronouns in e-mail signatures.
- Avoid gender-based language in programs and events. For example, if your library hosts a tea party for caregivers and their children, refrain from titles like *Tea for Mommy and Me* with a picture of a little girl and her mother. Something more inclusive

> could be *Tea for Two* with a variety of pictures of different people drinking tea.
>
> When communicating these ideas with staff, make sure that you do not require people to include their pronouns in e-mails or on name tags. For a variety of reasons, some people may not feel comfortable sharing their pronouns or gender identities. This should always be respected, and such practices should be optional. It is also crucial that your library develop strategies and policies that protect staff members from harassment and discrimination. We discuss this more in a later chapter.

Gender Expression

Gender expression is a separate concept from gender identity. While gender identity is private and personal, gender expression is how people communicate their gender publicly. This can be through clothing, appearance, and mannerisms. Society tends to interpret certain behaviors, roles, and characteristics as either masculine or feminine. As noted previously, this is dependent on culture. However, gender norms can also change over time.

For example, cheerleading in the United States was originally a male sport. Because most universities admitted only men, cheerleaders were often men from other sports who supported their peers. An article from 1911 describes the prestige of being a cheerleader:

> The reputation of having been a valiant "cheer-leader" is one of the most valuable things a boy can take away from college. As a title to promotion in professional or public life, it ranks hardly second to that of having been a quarterback.[8]

Today, 97 percent of cheerleaders are female athletes, and the support is often derided in popular culture.[9]

Beyond clothing, hair, and makeup, gender expression also manifests through a person's chosen name and pronouns. However, if someone does not feel safe or welcome to express their gender identity, they may present in ways that conform to societal expectations. As such, we should refrain from judgments about someone's gender identity based on how they present.

> ### GENDER NORMS THROUGH TIME
>
> Tights, dresses, heels, wigs, and the color pink are all examples of clothing styles that were originally created for or worn almost exclusively by men. Others were considered gender neutral. Now these items are considered feminine in much of the Western Hemisphere.
>
> Head over to the *Smithsonian*'s article "When Did Girls Start Wearing Pink?" by Jeanne Maglaty and read about the history of gendered children's clothing.* In the article you'll also see a picture of President Franklin Delano Roosevelt as a child. In the picture he has long, curly hair and is wearing a white, lacy dress. After, reflect on these questions:
>
> - What did you learn from this article?
> - How does this inform your understanding of sex, gender identity, and gender expression?
>
> *Jeanne Maglaty, "When Did Girls Start Wearing Pink?," *Smithsonian Magazine*, April 7, 2011, www.smithsonianmag.com/arts-culture/when-did-girls-start-wearing-pink-1370097/.

Sexual Orientation

You are likely familiar with the abbreviation LGBTQ, which stands for lesbian, gay, bisexual, transgender, and queer or questioning. (Note: in this book, I use the abbreviation LGBTQIA+, which includes "I" for intersex, "A" for asexual, and "+" for many other sexual and gender identities.) This tends to be a catch-all for people who are not heterosexual. But let's unpack this on a deeper level.

Sexual orientation describes a person's physical, romantic, and/or emotional attraction to another person. Historically, conversations related to sexual orientation have focused on "straight," "gay/lesbian," and "bi." Such conversations have a very narrow understanding of the

Part I: Foundation

breadth of sexual orientation. Here is a more comprehensive, albeit limited, overview of concepts related to sexual orientation:

- *Asexual* refers to someone who doesn't have sexual attraction or interest in sexual activity with others. Asexual individuals may still experience conditional sexual attraction.
- *Bisexual* applies to an individual who is emotionally, romantically, and/or sexually attracted to more than one gender.
- *Demisexual* refers to someone who experiences sexual attraction only after developing an emotional connection.
- *Gay* describes people who are emotionally, romantically, and/or sexually attracted to people of the same gender.
- *Lesbian* refers to a woman who is emotionally, romantically, and/or sexually attracted to other women.
- *Pansexual* describes someone whose emotional, romantic, and/or physical attraction is inclusive of people of all genders.
- *Questioning* refers to someone who is in the process of discovery and exploration about their sexual orientation, gender identity, gender expression, and so on. This can happen at any age and is a highly individualistic, important process.
- *Queer* is a word used by some members of the LGBTQIA+ community as an umbrella term to reclaim it and describe themselves. This word should be used to describe someone only with the expressed permission of someone who identifies as queer.
- *Heterosexual* describes people who are emotionally, romantically, and/or sexually attracted to people of a different gender or sex.

It is important to note that someone does not need to have sexual, emotional, or romantic experiences to identify with a sexual orientation. And although it is necessary to understand these different identities, it is also important that we do not label or make assumptions about another individual's sexual orientation. Instead, we should follow their lead in how they self-identify.

Sexuality and Health

Because sexuality deals with social norms, behaviors, and roles, people's access to and experiences with health care intersect with gender and sexual orientation. WHO explains that health care information, support, and services vary depending on one's gender. For instance, WHO notes that women and girls often face greater barriers than men and boys in accessing health information and services.[10] Gender bias in health care, including unconscious and implicit biases, may also impact clinician decision making.[11] WHO explains that gender inequality and discrimination can greatly impact one's health.[12]

Research has also found that members of the LGBTQIA+ community face societal stigma, violence, discrimination, and legislation that denies civil and human rights.[13] These can lead to health disparities that are further compounded for people who already have marginalized identities.

Intersectionality, a term coined by Dr. Kimberlé Crenshaw, describes a framework in which "systems of inequality based on gender, race, ethnicity, sexual orientation, gender identity, disability, class and other forms of discrimination 'intersect' to create unique dynamics and effects."[14] As Dr. Crenshaw explains,

> We tend to talk about race inequality as separate from inequality based on gender, class, sexuality, or immigrant status. What's often missing is how some people are subject to all of these, and the experience is not just the sum of its parts.[15]

This relates to health care and sexuality.

For instance, people of color, immigrants, low-income families, homeless people, and those with disabilities and mental health issues may face even more difficulties accessing comprehensive, unbiased health care. For example, someone may not be able to get the health care that they need because they do not have good—or any—insurance. Others may be limited in access to transportation, paid time off, child care, or technology to make and get to their appointments. Coupled with societal stigma, violence, discrimination, and inequitable legislation barriers are exacerbated. As such, we should keep intersectionality at the forefront of sexual and reproductive health when we build our collections, provide resources, and foster community relationships.

> ## INTERSECTIONALITY IN THE STACKS
>
> Watch Dr. Kimberlé Crenshaw's TED Talk, "The Urgency of Intersectionality."* After, reflect on these questions:
>
> - What types of materials and resources can you provide? Consider formats and languages.
> - How can you make these collections visible?
> - What relationships can you foster in your community that will make sexual and reproductive health more accessible?
>
> *Kimberlé Crenshaw, "The Urgency of Intersectionality," TED Talk, posted November 2016, https://www.ted.com/talks/kimberle_crenshaw_the_urgency_of_intersectionality.

Final Thoughts

Libraries can truly be a haven for people who need information related to sexuality. Not only can we create inclusive spaces that affirm human and civil rights, but we also can build comprehensive collections for SRH concepts. Information access can validate people's experiences and identities and provide people with tools and resources to help them navigate health care scenarios.

Let's Review

- Sexuality encompasses attitudes, values, and feelings that are influenced by both external and internal factors.
- Sex is a label that describes a child at birth based on their external anatomy, whereas gender refers to the social norms, behaviors, and roles that are given based on the sex a child is assigned at birth.
- Gender identity is how someone feels in relation to their gender. Gender expression is the external appearance of one's gender identity.

- Sexual orientation describes a person's physical, romantic, and/or emotional attraction to another person.
- Collections, resources, and community relationships should be developed with intersectionality in mind.

Reflection Questions

- How can you make the library a more inclusive space?
- What different types of community groups does your library serve? How can you ensure that sexual and reproductive health resources are inclusive to those groups?
- What actions can staff take to learn more about these concepts? (Trainings, book clubs, resource sharing?)

NOTES

1. "PFLAG National Glossary of Terms," PFLAG, updated June 2022, https://pflag.org/glossary.
2. "What Is Sexuality?," University of Louisville, https://louisville.edu/health promotion/elements-of-wellbeing/sexual-health-relationships/what-is-sexuality.
3. "Glossary of Terms," Human Rights Campaign (HRC), www.hrc.org/resources/glossary-of-terms.
4. "Gender and Health," World Health Organization (WHO), www.who.int/health-topics/gender#tab=tab_1.
5. "Glossary of Terms," HRC.
6. "Transgender and Non-binary People FAQ," Human Rights Campaign, www.hrc.org/resources/transgender-and-non-binary-faq.
7. "Glossary of Terms," HRC.
8. Karen Yuan and Caroline Kitchener, "How Cheerleading Went from Raucous and Male to Restrictive and Female," *The Atlantic,* April 27, 2018, www.theatlantic.com/membership/archive/2018/04/how-cheerleading-went-from-raucous-and-male-to-restrictive-and-female/559172/.
9. Elisabeth Sherman, "Why Don't More People Consider Cheerleading a Sport?," *The Atlantic,* May 2, 2017, www.theatlantic.com/entertainment/archive/2017/05/why-dont-more-people-consider-competitive-cheerleading-a-sport/524940/.

Part I: Foundation

10. "Gender and Health," WHO.
11. Jasmine R. Marcelin et al., "The Impact of Unconscious Bias in Healthcare: How to Recognize and Mitigate It," *The Journal of Infectious Diseases* 220, supp. 2 (2019): S62–S73, https://doi.org/10.1093/infdis/jiz214.
12. "Gender and Health," WHO.
13. "LGBT," Healthy People 2030, https://health.gov/healthypeople/objectives-and-data/browse-objectives/lgbt.
14. "What Is Intersectionality?," Center for Intersectional Justice, www.intersectionaljustice.org/what-is-intersectionality/.
15. Katy Steinmetz, "She Coined the Term 'Intersectionality' Over 30 Years Ago. Here's What It Means to Her Today," *Time,* February 20, 2020, https://time.com/5786710/kimberle-crenshaw-intersectionality/.

PART II

Education

By now we have a firm awareness of the overall concepts related to sexual and reproductive health, including how this specifically relates to public libraries. So now let's move on to specifics about sexual and reproductive health. The next three chapters provide key definitions, relevant US-based legislation, and suggestions for reference interviews, collection development, and library services.

CHAPTER FOUR

Sexual Health

SEXUAL HEALTH IS a public health issue that is often shrouded in stigma and shame. For example, patrons may not necessarily be nervous about asking a librarian for information about preventing heart disease, but they will probably be nervous to ask a librarian for information about preventing pregnancy. As librarians, we have an opportunity to create a welcoming library environment that is robust with comprehensive resources to aid people in their search strategies. By doing so, we can contribute to health equity in our communities.

Overview of Sexual Health

So far we have talked about sexual health and reproductive health in tandem. As a reminder, sexual and reproductive health "implies that people are able to have a satisfying and safe sex life and have the capability to reproduce and the freedom to decide if, when, and how often to do so."[1]

But let's break down that concept by focusing on solely sexual health. The World Health Organization (WHO), which has conducted sexual health work since 1974, has some core definitions related to sexual health. These definitions were developed through consultation with key experts from the World Association for Sexual Health (WAS) and the Pan American Health Organization (PAHO).[2] As outlined by WHO, the main conceptual elements of sexual health include the following:

- Sexual health is about well-being, not merely the absence of disease.
- Sexual health involves respect, safety and freedom from discrimination and violence.
- Sexual health depends on the fulfilment of certain human rights.
- Sexual health is relevant throughout the individual's lifespan, not only to those in the reproductive years, but also to both the young and the elderly.
- Sexual health is expressed through diverse sexualities and forms of sexual expression.
- Sexual health is critically influenced by gender norms, roles, expectations and power dynamics.[3]

And although sexual health has typically been a conversation focused on risk and adverse outcomes, scholars are continuously considering a new lens for approaching sexual health. For example, an academic article published in *Lancet Public Health* introduces four pillars of a comprehensive public health approach to sexuality: sexual health, sexual pleasure, sexual well-being, and sexual justice (see figure 4.1). Specifically focusing on sexual well-being, the authors argue that it is imperative for public health because it is a marker of health equity, a population indicator of well-being, and holistically focuses on communities and context.[4]

Sexual Health Concepts

Specifically, this chapter includes information about contraception, sterilization, sexually transmitted infections, sexual pleasure and consent, sexual violence, and sexual harassment. Obviously, there is much more to discuss regarding sexual health, but for the purposes of this book, we focus on these core areas. Let's begin!

Contraception

Also known as birth control, contraception is a method for preventing pregnancy and is hardly a new concept. In fact, in ancient Egypt, people

FIGURE 4.1

Four pillars of comprehensive public health focused inquiry and intervention in relation to sexuality

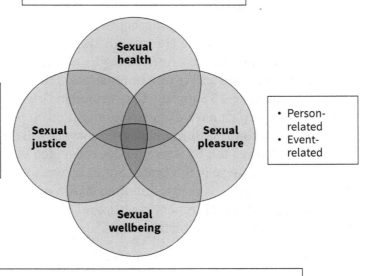

Source: Image from Kirstin R. Mitchell, Ruth Lewis, Lucia F. O'Sullivan, and J. Dennis Fortenberry, "What Is Sexual Wellbeing and Why Does It Matter for Public Health?," *The Lancet Public Health* 6, no. 8 (2021): E608–E613, https://doi.org/10.1016/S2468-2667(21)00099-2. Image licensed under a CC BY 4.0 license (https://creativecommons.org/licenses/by/4.0/) and has been adapted for print in black and white.

used a paste made out of honey, sodium carbonate, and crocodile dung as a form of contraception.[5]

Specifically in the United States, antiobscenity laws in the nineteenth and twentieth centuries prevented doctors from spreading information about contraception. In fact, the Comstock Act, a federal law passed in 1873, made it a federal offense to share information about birth control through the mail or across state lines. It wasn't until 1936 that the US Circuit Court of Appeals in *United States v. One Package* determined that doctors could distribute contraceptives across state lines.[6] By 1939, almost 400 community-based and state-sponsored birth control clinics were developed in the United States. Two years later, the National Council of Negro Women became the first national women's organization to officially endorse contraception as a legitimate practice.

Meanwhile, the first oral contraceptive was tested on patients in the Worcester State Psychiatric Hospital in Massachusetts and on low-income women in Puerto Rico. And although oral contraceptives had been approved by the Food and Drug Administration (FDA) in 1960, it wasn't until 1965 when the US Supreme Court ruled in *Griswold v. Connecticut* that married couples have a constitutional right to privacy, including the use of birth control. Unmarried women were still denied birth control until 1972 when the US Supreme Court decided *Eisenstadt v. Baird*.[7]

Birth control is legal in the United States in a variety of forms. People may choose their birth control method based on numerous factors, including personal preference, health, and sexual activity. These are the most popular types of birth control:[8]

- barriers: condoms, diaphragms, cervical caps, and contraceptive sponges
- hormonal methods: birth control pills, patches, shots, vaginal rings, and emergency contraceptive pills
- long-acting reversible contraception (LARC): intrauterine devices (IUDs) and birth control implants that can be inserted in the uterus or arm for several years
- emergency contraception (EC): not a regular form of birth control; a pill that can be taken up to five days after intercourse to prevent pregnancy; may be used in situations where contraception wasn't used, failed, or was used incorrectly[9]

Presently, barrier birth control and EC can be accessed in drugstores and health departments. Hormonal and LARC options are typically available only with a doctor's prescription. Depending on the state in which your library resides, minors may be allowed to access certain contraceptives without parental consent.[10]

Sterilization

So far, we have talked about temporary forms of birth control. Sterilization is a type of permanent birth control. Tubal ligations and vasectomies are two of the most popular types of sterilization procedures.

- A tubal ligation closes off the fallopian tubes through cutting, tying, or blocking. This prevents the egg from moving through the fallopian tube and blocks sperm from reaching the egg.
- In a vasectomy, the vas deferens tubes are tied, cut, clipped, and sealed to prevent the release of sperm into the semen.

Both procedures are highly effective at preventing pregnancy. However, sterilization has a checkered history and continues to have a complicated present. For instance, many people also seek voluntary sterilization as a form of family planning. According to the American College of Obstetricians and Gynecologists, sterilization is "the most common method of contraception among married couples, with nearly twice as many couples choosing female partner sterilization over male sterilization."[11] Nevertheless, women often receive more pushback than men when requesting sterilization. One article stated that women in Canada and the United States are often told "You'll regret it" or "Get your husband to do it" because vasectomies are reversible whereas tubal ligations are not.[12] In fact, one person tweeted that she couldn't get a tubal ligation without her husband's signature.[13] According to the Guttmacher Institute, health care practitioners in eighteen states can refuse to provide sterilization services.[14] This means that access to information about sterilization, particularly in public libraries, is crucial.

> **"THE WORLD ALREADY HAS TOO MANY PEOPLE IN IT!"**
>
> When discussing sterilization, birth control, and abortion, you may hear of people whose primary concern is the environment or overpopulation. Some people may say that "we already have too many people in this world" or "we need to stop reproducing to protect the environment." These are problematic concepts as they put the blame on the individual,

Part II: Education

> rather than on a system that has the means, resources, and money to protect the environment but chooses not to do so.
>
> Furthermore, this logic is counter to reproductive justice, which defends the rights of people to choose to have children, to choose not to have children, and to raise their children in healthy environments. Because research has shown that poor communities are exposed to elevated levels of air pollution and other environmental concerns,* discussion about the environment and population growth is best centered around raising families in communities with clear air, fresh water, and quality food—not restricting their ability to family plan.
>
> *Tara Failey, "Poor Communities Exposed to Elevated Air Pollution Levels," *Global Environmental Health Newsletter,* April 2016, www.niehs.nih.gov/research/programs/geh/geh_newsletter/2016/4/spotlight/poor_communities_exposed_to_elevated_air_pollution_levels.cfm.

Sexually Transmitted Infections

According to WHO, more than 1 million sexually transmitted infections (STIs) are acquired every day worldwide. The majority of STIs are asymptomatic—meaning that they have no symptoms. STIs are an important area of sexual health as they are often associated with confusion and shame. This may prevent people from seeking information altogether or lead to their not turning to credible resources.

STIs are nothing new. In fact, researchers have determined that clay tablets from Mesopotamia, Egyptian papyri, and mythology have demonstrated the presence of STIs in the ancient world.[15] The CDC provides a timeline for the evolution of STI treatment (see figure 4.2). According to the CDC, penicillin was used to treat and cure syphilis for the first time in 1943, and consequently penicillin became the standard treatment for STIs throughout the 1950s. The first STI training center model clinic was established in 1979, and the CDC's first comprehensive treatment guidelines for STIs were published in 1982.[16] As such, science-backed STI treatment is a new and revolutionary concept.

More than thirty different bacteria, viruses, and parasites are transmitted through sexual contact, including vaginal, anal, and oral sex.

Chapter Four: Sexual Health

FIGURE 4.2
CDC's STI Treatment Guidelines Timeline: The Evolution of Sexual Healthcare

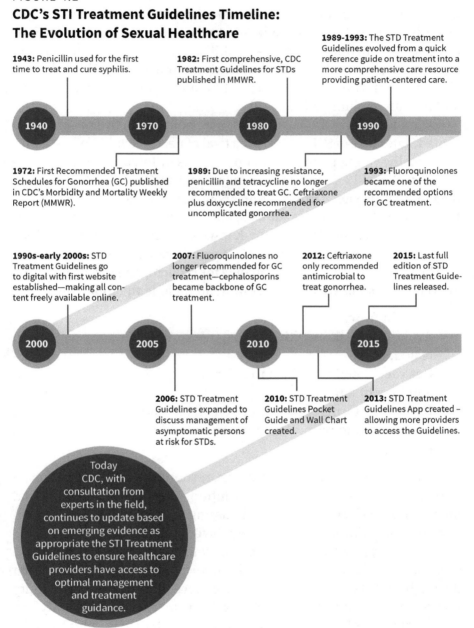

Source: Centers for Disease Control and Prevention, "CDC's STI Treatment Guidelines Timeline: The Evolution of Sexual Healthcare," last reviewed August 2, 2021, www.cdc.gov/std/treatment-guidelines/timeline.htm.

Some STIs can also be transmitted during pregnancy, childbirth, and breastfeeding or through blood transfusions and shared needles. Specifically, eight pathogens are linked to the most prevalent STIs. Four of these are currently curable—syphilis, gonorrhea, chlamydia, and trichomoniasis—while four are currently incurable—hepatitis B, herpes simplex virus (HSV or herpes), HIV (human immunodeficiency virus), and human papillomavirus (HPV).[17]

Estimates by the CDC have found that about one in five people in the United States had an STI in 2018, for a total of nearly 68 million infections. Specifically, young people between the ages of fifteen and twenty-five made up almost 13 million of the newly acquired STIs in 2018.[18] However, older adults also need information about STIs. In a study that screened for STI knowledge among adults aged sixty-five to ninety-four, results found that older adults had low knowledge scores regarding STIs.[19] Essentially, information about STIs is a multigenerational necessity.

The Mayo Clinic provides guidance for reducing the risk of acquiring an STI.[20] The steps that they recommend include the following:

- Abstain from sex.
- Avoid intercourse with new partners until you both have been tested.
- Get vaccinated to reduce the risk of acquiring HPV, hepatitis A, and hepatitis B.
- Use barrier forms of contraception, like condoms and dental dams.
- Communicate with your partner about boundaries and sexual history.

As such, the library can provide books, resources, and programs on all of these different areas of STI prevention. However, the truth is that many people feel stigmatized for discussing STIs or seeking information and treatment. In fact, researchers have found that many emerging adults, or people between ages eighteen and twenty-five, do not disclose their status to a partner, seek social support, or get tested. Results from the study found that emerging adults believe that "if their community found out they got tested, they would likely be treated differently."[21]

Perhaps one of the most stigmatized STIs is HIV. HIV, which had its first cases reported in 1981, is a virus that attacks the body's immune system. If left untreated, HIV can lead to acquired immunodeficiency syndrome (AIDS). Presently, there is no cure for HIV, although medical advances mean that people who receive effective treatment can live long and healthy lives.[22]

Nevertheless, stigma surrounding HIV has proliferated for more than forty years. And while anyone can acquire HIV, members of the LGBTQIA+ community are disproportionately impacted. As the Human Rights Campaign explains, "Insufficient funding for public health programs, ideological opposition to common sense prevention policies, and societal barriers like stigma and discrimination" only amplify these inequalities.[23] In fact, an article in *AMA Journal of Ethics* noted that despite legal protections, people with HIV are "denied and fired from jobs, kicked out of residences, ordered to limit contact with family, and discriminated against in many other ways because they have HIV."[24]

Libraries can play an important role in providing not only information in a safe space but also resources to reduce STI stigma and help people communicate about sexual health.

Sexual Pleasure and Consent

As previously noted, WHO describes sexual health as being "about well-being, not merely the absence of disease," as well as encompassing "respect, safety and freedom from discrimination and violence."[25] Essentially, sexual health isn't just about understanding STIs and birth control options. It also includes emotional, mental, and psychological aspects of health. This includes sexual pleasure.

The American Sexual Health Association defines sexual pleasure as an enjoyment of certain sexual behaviors and practices. Sexual pleasure can be achieved by oneself or with a consenting partner. Communication about boundaries, preferences, health, needs, and responsibilities is key to a satisfying sex life.[26]

Providing information and resources about pleasure, consent, and healthy relationship communication is crucial. Consent is defined as "an agreement between participants to engage in sexual activity."[27] Consent cannot be given by people who are underage, intoxicated, incapacitated by drugs or alcohol, asleep, or unconscious. Most important, consent can be withdrawn at any point and is not contingent upon sexual activities done in the past.[28]

Part II: Education

SEX EDUCATION IN SCHOOLS

As public librarians, we have opportunities to fill in the gaps or to complement the existing curricula in our libraries' school districts. To determine where our efforts are most needed, let's take a look at some core legislation related to sex education.

To date, thirty-eight states and the District of Columbia mandate sex education and/or HIV education. Only seventeen states require that the content be medically accurate, and only ten states require that the education not be "biased against any race, sex, or ethnicity."[*] Related to actual content, twenty-nine states require that abstinence be emphasized, and three states require that only heteronormative sex be discussed positively. In terms of parental consent, thirty-five states and the District of Columbia allow parents the option to remove their child from instruction about sex education.

Furthermore, only nineteen states require inclusion of information about condoms and contraception, and only twenty-seven states require instruction on self-control and decision making about sexuality. Regarding sexual violence and teen dating violence, a mere eleven states require the importance of consent to sexual activity to be covered, and twenty-four states require information about personal boundaries and refusing unwanted sexual advances.

Additionally, 19 percent of people in the United States live in a state with an LGBTQIA+ curriculum ban. In 2022, at least twenty states have introduced "Don't Say Gay" legislation that prevents schoolteachers from discussing LGBTQIA+ people or history in public elementary schools.[†] You can see how your state legislates at Movement Advancement Project (https://www.lgbtmap.org/equality-maps/curricular_laws).

It may be helpful for you to review your state's laws and policies regarding sex education. Furthermore, you may want to consider connecting with local schools and reviewing their sex education curricula. These steps can help you determine what areas of your collection are most needed.

[*]"Sex and HIV Education," Guttmacher Institute, November 1, 2022, https://www.guttmacher.org/state-policy/explore/sex-and-hiv-education?gclid=CjwKCAjwo8-SBhAlEiwAopc9W5B3b2KdahhlifmfRslcRFZwKpYeIBnnb6_4Au9k7rJ-9su71Uq1ORoCh7wQAvD_BwE

[†]Kate Sosin, "'Don't Say Gay' Bills Aren't New. They've Just Been Revived," The 19th, April 20, 2022, https://19thnews.org/2022/04/dont-say-gay-existed-before-florida-alabama-laws/.

Sexual Violence

Sexual violence, including sexual abuse, is defined as sexual activity when consent is not obtained or freely given. It can impact people of all sexual orientations, genders, and ages. Furthermore, sexual violence can occur both in person or online. For example, nonconsensual sexting or sharing sexual pictures without consent is a form of sexual violence. Furthermore, researchers from UCLA have determined that members of the LGBTQIA+ community are nearly four times more likely to experience "violent victimization, including rape, sexual assault, and aggravated or simple assault."[29]

Contrary to popular representation, sexual violence does not overwhelmingly involve strangers attacking random people in dark alleys. Rather, it is most often perpetrated by people whom the survivor knows. According to RAINN, the Rape, Abuse, and Incest National Network, eight out of ten rapes are committed by someone known to the survivor.[30] According to the CDC, nearly 35 percent of female rape survivors and almost 30 percent of male rape survivors were victimized for the first time between the ages of eleven and seventeen.[31] The impact of sexual violence is chronic and is linked to post-traumatic stress disorder as well as "re-occurring reproductive, gastrointestinal, cardiovascular, and sexual health problems."[32] Furthermore, girls who are sexually abused are more likely to become victims of intimate partner violence in adulthood.[33]

Recent discourse and action regarding consent and sexual violence first formed in 2006 when Tarana Burke founded the Me Too movement in order to "support survivors of sexual violence, particularly young women of color from low-wealth communities, to find pathways to healing."[34] Since then, the #MeToo initiative has grown, becoming a global movement in October 2017.[35] The #MeToo movement has propelled new legislation guarding against sexual violence. In fact, fifteen states have passed new laws protecting against sexual harassment in the workplace, and some states—like New York, Illinois, and California—have laws that mandate sexual harassment training.[36]

And yet there is still much work to be done. Survivors of sexual violence are often marginalized by legislation and society. For example, it wasn't until 1993 that marital rape became a crime in all fifty states. Prior to that, marital rape wasn't considered to be "real rape" even though roughly 14 percent of married women are raped by their husbands in the United States.[37] And even still there are legal loopholes in some states that do not criminalize marital rape.[38] Furthermore, researchers from the University of California–Davis found data that indicates a surge in intimate partner violence (IPV) during the COVID-19 pandemic. The study found not only that stressors like income loss, nutritional stress, and rental concerns increased the likelihood of IPV but also that survivors had limited communication methods to seek help.[39]

This lends the library opportunities to provide books, materials, and community partnerships for patrons of all ages about boundaries and bodily autonomy. Beyond providing information, it is also important to provide resources about where survivors can seek help and speak to professionals. A good starting place would be to partner with a local or regional organization that focuses on helping survivors of sexual and domestic violence. Consider sharing their informational materials and hosting programs and informational sessions with such organizations. You may also want to provide a resource guide with information about hotlines and organizations that people can connect with confidentially.

SEXUAL VIOLENCE PREVENTION INFORMATION

As a librarian, I have seen books about sexual harassment that focus solely on "tips" for avoiding sexual violence. I've been shocked to see some books that still dictate what someone should wear, when they should or should not be by themselves, and where they can or cannot go. Such books are counterproductive because they not only put blame on the victim instead of the aggressor but also are incongruent with statistics showing that sexual violence is most likely done by someone the victim knows and can happen regardless of what a person is wearing or where they are walking. Be mindful of these books, resources, and programs, and consider how you can incorporate books that are not accusatory. A resource that you may want to explore for your community is *STOP SV: A Technical Package to Prevent Sexual Violence,* developed by the CDC (https://www.cdc.gov/violenceprevention/sexualviolence/fastfact.html). It is available in both English and Spanish.

Sexual Harassment in the Library

Librarians are not immune from sexual harassment. In fact, a study found that sexual harassment in academic libraries is frequent, with 64 percent of people reporting that they have experienced inappropriate behavior by patrons and 35 percent that they have experienced sexual assault.[40]

Certainly, some patrons ask vulgar questions to get a rise out of librarians at the desk. Let's be clear: just because we provide sexual and reproductive health information does not mean that we should be subjected to questions that are unprofessional, rude, or inappropriate or that make us uncomfortable. Additionally, as librarians, our goal is to direct people to resources—not interpret material for them. This means that if a patron wants you to describe or interpret sexual health material, refuse to do so. I highly encourage you and your management team to develop clear policies that protect staff and other patrons from harassment. Management should give staff full support in creating an environment where sexual harassment is not tolerated.

Developing practices for dealing with sexual harassment can also be helpful. One of the most impactful practices that colleagues and I implemented was something we referred to as "The Color System." Using the colors green, yellow, and red, we alerted our colleagues if we were in a situation that felt uncomfortable. Yellow signaled that we felt the situation escalating and needed support from a colleague. So, for example, if I began to feel uncomfortable with a patron, I would say to a colleague who was walking by the desk, "Can you help me find that yellow book?" This would alert the colleague to get support and to stick near me at the desk. If the situation did escalate, I would have a colleague nearby who could come to my aid.

This same situation played out with the color red, except that red meant that I was in a more intense situation and needed either the director or the librarian in charge immediately. This strategy could also be implemented via e-mail or staff chat or by phone if a colleague was not passing by. All staff members were trained on this procedure, and it was also included in all staff procedural manuals and placed on the staff side of every service desk. This model helped create an environment where we felt that we could trust one another and were empowered to come up with other solutions for staff safety.

Final Thoughts

This chapter discusses a lot of crucial information related to sexual health. Perhaps the biggest takeaway from this chapter is that silence emboldens stigma, shame, and violence. Whether it is related to preventing unwanted pregnancies, seeking treatment for an STI, or seeking support after a sexual assault, people should never feel that they cannot turn to the library for the information that they need. I encourage you to dive into the recommended books, articles, media, and resources provided in the appendix so that you can continue to learn about how these issues directly impact the lives of your patrons.

Let's Review

- There are myriad ways that contraception can help someone avoid a pregnancy and/or an STI. Depending on the form of contraception, people may be able to access it in a drugstore or via a doctor's prescription.
- STIs are very common but heavily stigmatized. This may prevent people from seeking help or speaking effectively with partners and family members.
- Sexual violence is an issue related to sexual health that must not be ignored. Public libraries can build a library culture and collection that advocates for consent and communication.

Reflection Questions

1. What is your biggest takeaway from the discussion of how you can provide information about contraception and STIs?
2. How can you work with the local school district to determine the gaps that you can fill related to sex education?
3. What are three ways that your library can support survivors of sexual violence and build a culture of consent?

Chapter Four: Sexual Health

NOTES

1. "Sexual and Reproductive Health," United Nations Population Fund, www.unfpa.org/sexual-reproductive-health.
2. "Defining Sexual Health," World Health Organization (WHO), www.who.int/teams/sexual-and-reproductive-health-and-research/key-areas-of-work/sexual-health/defining-sexual-health.
3. "Defining Sexual Health," WHO.
4. Kirstin R. Mitchell et al., "What Is Sexual Wellbeing and Why Does It Matter for Public Health?," *The Lancet Public Health* 6, no. 8 (2021): E608–E613, https://doi.org/10.1016/S2468-2667(21)00099-2.
5. Ciro Comparetto and Franco Borruto, "The History of Contraception: From Ancient Egyptians to the 'Morning After,'" ResearchGate, January 2014, www.researchgate.net/publication/293071233_The_history_of_contraception_From_ancient_egyptians_to_the_morning_after.
6. "Anthony Comstock's 'Chastity' Laws," American Experience, PBS, www.pbs.org/wgbh/americanexperience/features/pill-anthony-comstocks-chastity-laws/.
7. "A Brief History of Birth Control in the U.S.," Our Bodies Ourselves Today, www.ourbodiesourselves.org/book-excerpts/health-article/a-brief-history-of-birth-control/.
8. "Birth Control," MedlinePlus, National Library of Medicine, last updated August 12, 2022, https://medlineplus.gov/birthcontrol.html.
9. "Emergency Contraception," World Health Organization, November 9, 2021, www.who.int/news-room/fact-sheets/detail/emergency-contraception.
10. "Minor's Access to Contraceptive Services," Guttmacher Institute, as of September 1, 2022, www.guttmacher.org/state-policy/explore/minors-access-contraceptive-services.
11. "Sterilization of Women: Ethical Issues and Considerations," American College of Obstetricians and Gynecologists, April 2017, www.acog.org/clinical/clinical-guidance/committee-opinion/articles/2017/04/sterilization-of-women-ethical-issues-and-considerations.
12. Dianne Lalonde, "Sexist Barriers Block Women's Choice to Be Sterilized," The Conversation, August 14, 2018, https://theconversation.com/sexist-barriers-block-womens-choice-to-be-sterilized-99754.
13. Shira Feder, "A Woman Was Told She Needed Her Husband's Permission to Get Her Tubes Tied. Her Story Went Viral, but It's Not Uncommon," Insider, February 25, 2020, www.insider.com/a-woman-needed-husbands-consent-to-get-her-tubes-tied-2020-2.

Part II: Education

14. "Refusing to Provide Health Services," Guttmacher Institute, as of September 1, 2022, www.guttmacher.org/state-policy/explore/refusing-provide-health-services.
15. Franjo Gruber, Jasna Lipozenčić, and Tatjana Kehler, "History of Venereal Diseases from Antiquity to the Renaissance," *Acta dermatovenerologica Croatica: ADC* 23, no. 1 (2015): 1–11.
16. "CDC's STI Treatment Guidelines Timeline: The Evolution of Sexual Healthcare," Centers for Disease Control and Prevention, last reviewed August 2, 2021, www.cdc.gov/std/treatment-guidelines/timeline.htm.
17. "Sexually Transmitted Infections (STIs)," World Health Organization, August 22, 2022, www.who.int/news-room/fact-sheets/detail/sexually-transmitted-infections-(stis).
18. "STI Prevalence, Incidence, and Cost Estimates," Centers for Disease Control and Prevention, last reviewed February 18, 2021, www.cdc.gov/std/statistics/prevalence-incidence-cost-2020.htm.
19. Matthew L. Smith et al., "Sexually Transmitted Infection Knowledge among Older Adults: Psychometrics and Test-Retest Reliability," *International Journal of Environmental Research and Public Health* 17, no. 7 (2020): 2462, https://doi.org/10.3390/ijerph17072462.
20. "Sexually Transmitted Diseases (STDs)—Symptoms and Causes," Mayo Clinic, September 21, 2021, www.mayoclinic.org/diseases-conditions/sexually-transmitted-diseases-stds/symptoms-causes/syc-20351240.
21. Emily Scheinfeld, "Shame and STIs: An Exploration of Emerging Adult Students' Felt Shame and Stigma towards Getting Tested for and Disclosing Sexually Transmitted Infections," *International Journal of Environmental Research and Public Health* 18, no. 13 (2021): 7179, https://doi.org/10.3390/ijerph18137179.
22. "About HIV/AIDS," Centers for Disease Control and Prevention, last reviewed June 30, 2022, www.cdc.gov/hiv/basics/whatishiv.html.
23. "How HIV Impacts LGBTQ People," Human Rights Campaign, last updated February 2017, www.hrc.org/resources/hrc-issue-brief-hiv-aids-and-the-lgbt-community.
24. Bebe J. Anderson, "HIV Stigma and Discrimination Persist, Even in Health Care," *AMA Journal of Ethics,* December 1, 2009, https://journalofethics.ama-assn.org/article/hiv-stigma-and-discrimination-persist-even-health-care/2009-12.

25. "Defining Sexual Health," WHO.
26. "Sexual Pleasure," American Sexual Health Association, www.ashasexualhealth.org/your-sexual-pleasure/.
27. "What Consent Looks Like," RAINN, www.rainn.org/articles/what-is-consent.
28. "What Consent Looks Like," RAINN.
29. Williams Institute School of Law, "LGBT People Nearly Four Times More Likely Than Non-LGBT People to Be Victims of Violent Crime," Williams Institute, October 2, 2020, https://williamsinstitute.law.ucla.edu/press/ncvs-lgbt-violence-press-release/.
30. "Perpetrators of Sexual Violence: Statistics," RAINN, www.rainn.org/statistics/perpetrators-sexual-violence.
31. Kathleen C. Basile et al., *National Intimate Partner and Sexual Violence Survey: 2016/2017 Report on Sexual Violence* (Atlanta, GA: National Center for Injury Prevention and Control, Centers for Disease Control and Prevention, 2002), https://www.cdc.gov/violenceprevention/pdf/nisvs/nisvsReportonSexualViolence.pdf.
32. "Fast Facts: Preventing Sexual Violence," Centers for Disease Control and Prevention, last reviewed June 22, 2022, www.cdc.gov/violenceprevention/sexualviolence/fastfact.html.
33. "Fast Facts: Preventing Sexual Violence," CDC.
34. "'Me Too.' Global Movement," Global Fund for Women, www.globalfundforwomen.org/movements/me-too/.
35. "'Me Too.' Global Movement," Global Fund for Women.
36. Erik A. Christiansen, "How Are the Laws Sparked by #MeToo Affecting Workplace Harassment?," American Bar Association, May 8, 2020, https://www.americanbar.org/groups/litigation/publications/litigation-news/featured-articles/2020/new-state-laws-expand-workplace-protections-sexual-harassment-victims.
37. "Marital Rape: New Research and Directions," VAWnet, February 2006, https://vawnet.org/material/marital-rape-new-research-and-directions.
38. Misha Valencia, "Marital Rape Is Still Legal," HealthyWomen, June 2, 2021, www.healthywomen.org/your-care/marital-rape/particle-1.
39. Clare E. B. Cannon et al., "COVID-19, Intimate Partner Violence, and Communication Ecologies," *American Behavioral Scientist* 65, no. 7 (2021): 992–1013, https://doi.org/10.1177/0002764221992826.

Part II: Education

40. Ally Dever, "#MeToo: Study Finds Sexual Harassment in Academic Libraries More Frequent Than Thought," CU Boulder Today, September 2, 2021, www.colorado.edu/today/2021/09/02/metoo-study-finds-sexual-harassment-academic-libraries-more-frequent-thought.

CHAPTER FIVE

Reproductive Health

WHEN WE BETTER understand reproductive health issues, we can build stronger collections and provide better reference interviews. This chapter explores the core areas of reproductive health. It is not exhaustive but instead meant to be a grounding guide. Please note the recommended resources in the appendix that expand upon these concepts. Let's dive in!

Overview of Reproductive Health

Reproductive health is defined as a state of physical, mental, and social well-being in all matters related to the reproductive system and at all stages of life. It further means that people have access to information and resources so that they can have satisfying and safe sex lives and the capability to reproduce (or not reproduce) on their own terms.[1]

As we've discussed earlier in this book, reproductive justice is an important framework when discussing sexual and reproductive health. Reproductive justice hinges on the human right to control one's life, including one's sexuality and reproduction. However, many barriers prevent one from being able to have total control over one's reproductive destiny. To be sure, political, economic, legislative, and social factors play major roles in creating a world where one has total autonomy over one's body, identity, and reproductive health. I believe that information access—or lack thereof—also plays a major role in working toward reproductive health. One is not able to make decisions or seek services

Part II: Education

if one is unaware of core concepts. This means that information access is key to achieving reproductive health.

Reproductive Health Concepts

There is a wide range of concepts in this area, but we will focus on some of the most popular issues that may come our way in the library. I encourage you to see this as an introductory section and to lean on the resources for continued education and information.

Menstruation

Menstruation is the monthly shedding of uterine lining when fertilization has not occurred. This results in vaginal bleeding and is often referred to as a period. Menarche, or the onset of menstruation, typically begins between the ages of eleven and fourteen but can occur anytime from nine to seventeen years of age.[2] The onset of menstruation can be a very scary or unnerving process for some. The library can provide books, magazines, and resources about menstruation.

Menstrual cycles, or the first day of one period to the first day of the next, can vary in length between twenty-one and thirty-five days. Ovulation, or release of an egg from the ovaries into the fallopian tubes, occurs around the fourteenth day before the next period. If fertilization does not occur, the uterine lining is shed, resulting in menstruation. Medication and medical devices, including birth control pills and IUDs, may change the menstrual cycle, stop ovulation, and prevent pregnancy. In fact, some people may purposefully take hormonal birth control to temporarily halt their periods, alleviate symptoms of menstrual pain, and protect themselves against pregnancy.

Amenorrhea is defined as the absence of menstruation and is broken down into two basic categories: primary amenorrhea and secondary amenorrhea. Primary amenorrhea is when someone has not gotten their period by age fifteen. Secondary amenorrhea is when someone has stopped having regular menstrual periods for more than a few months, excusing pregnancy, breastfeeding, or menopause.[3]

Menstrual pain, or dysmenorrhea, is extremely common. Research published in the *Journal of Pain Research* found that 84.1 percent of

Chapter Five: Reproductive Health

women reported experiencing menstrual pain, with 43.1 percent reporting pain that occurs every period and 41 percent reporting pain that occurs in some periods.[4] It is important to note that dysmenorrhea can be further divided into two categories: primary and secondary dysmenorrhea. The previous descriptions are typical in primary dysmenorrhea, whereas secondary dysmenorrhea refers to pain that lasts longer, is more severe than normal menstrual cramps, and gets worse as the period continues. These symptoms may be caused by endometriosis, fibroids, adenomyosis, or other conditions affecting the reproductive organs.[5]

Dysmenorrhea negatively affects one's quality of daily life. Research published in *BMC Women's Health* found that some of these negative factors are a leading cause of absence from school and work and are associated with other pain conditions like migraines, fibromyalgia, and irritable bowel syndrome. Despite these painful experiences, study participants often did not view dysmenorrhea as a legitimate health issue. Rather, they felt that health care providers, employers, and society did not see period pain as a legitimate problem and had "little sympathy" for it.[6]

MENSTRUAL INTERRUPTIONS AND ABSENCE

As important as it is to have information on menstruation, it is also crucial to have information about conditions that may cause someone to miss or never have a menstrual period.

Polycystic ovary syndrome (PCOS) is a hormonal condition in which someone may have interrupted menstrual periods related to hormonal imbalances. Treatment may include hormonal birth control or other medication to manage hormones. Learn more at the website of the American College of Obstetricians and Gynecologists (www.acog.org).

Androgen insensitivity syndrome (AIS) is when someone has XY chromosomes but is resistant to androgens, male sex hormones. You can learn more at the website of Accord Alliance (www.accordalliance.org).

Turner syndrome occurs when one of the X chromosomes is missing or partially missing. This may result in the loss of ovarian functions.

Part II: Education

> Someone with Turner syndrome may require hormone therapy. You can learn more at the Cleveland Clinic website (https://my.clevelandclinic.org/health/diseases/15200-turner-syndrome).

Perimenopause and Menopause

Menopause marks the end of one's menstrual cycles and is a result of the ovaries making less estrogen and progesterone. It is typically diagnosed after one goes twelve months without a menstrual period, and most often happens in one's forties and fifties. The average age of menopause is fifty-one years old in the United States. Symptoms may include hot flashes, chills, night sweats, lower energy, sleep disruption, and mood changes. However, it can also result from surgical removal of the ovaries. Chemotherapy and radiation therapy can also induce menopause. Hormone therapy and different medications can help alleviate symptoms.[7]

Perimenopause is defined as the time when the body begins to make the transition to menopause. Some people may start to notice changes in their midthirties. Irregular periods, hot flashes, mood changes, loss of bone, changing cholesterol levels, and vaginal and bladder problems are some symptoms of perimenopause.[8]

Approaching and going through menopause can be a confusing time—both physically and emotionally. Resources to help people identify, communicate, and navigate menopause are necessary for a comprehensive sexual and reproductive health collection.

MENSTRUATION AS A HUMAN RIGHTS ISSUE

Did you know that one in five girls in the United States misses school because she can't afford menstrual products? Furthermore, 25 million women in the United States live in poverty, but food stamps do not cover menstrual products.* These numbers do not account for transmen and nonbinary people who also may be forced to go without adequate menstrual products. Beyond this, period products are subject to taxes in thirty states because they are deemed nonessential items.† These concepts directly correlate to period poverty, or the phenomenon of people being unable to afford menstrual products like pads, tampons, liners, or menstrual cups to manage menstrual bleeding.‡

The United Nations has declared menstruation to be a human rights issue, explaining that "menstruation is intrinsically related to human dignity—when people cannot access safe bathing facilities and safe and effective means of managing their menstrual hygiene, they are not able to manage their menstruation with dignity."§ This impacts one's right to health, education, work, gender equality, water, and sanitation. Learn more at the United Nations Population Fund's "Menstruation and Human Rights" webpage (www.unfpa.org/menstruationfaq). In a later chapter, we will discuss menstrual justice at the library.

*Regis College Online, "Period Poverty, Stigma, and Female Hygiene Gaps in the U.S. and Around the World," October 28, 2021, https://online.regiscollege.edu/blog/period-poverty/.

†L. Rodriguez, "The Tampon Tax: Everything You Need to Know," *Global Citizen*, June 28, 2021, www.globalcitizen.org/en/content/tampon-tax-explained-definition-facts-statistics/.

‡Ashley Rapp and Sidonie Kilpatrick, "Changing the Cycle: Period Poverty as a Public Health Crisis," University of Michigan, February 4, 2020, https://sph.umich.edu/pursuit/2020posts/period-poverty.html.

§"Menstruation and Human Rights: Frequently Asked Questions—How is menstruation related to human rights?," United Nations Population Fund, May 2022, https://www.unfpa.org/menstruationfaq.

Endometriosis, Uterine Fibroids, and Adenomyosis

According to Johns Hopkins, the most common cause of secondary dysmenorrhea is endometriosis, or a condition in which endometrial tissue implants outside the uterus. This can cause internal bleeding, infection, and pelvic pain.[9] Researchers estimate that more than 6.5 million women in the United States have endometriosis. It is especially common for women in their thirties and forties. Hormonal birth control methods, such as birth control pills, the birth control shot, or IUDs, are often recommended as treatment. Surgical procedures may also be recommended for treatment in more severe cases.[10]

Uterine fibroids can also cause irregular periods and discomfort. Uterine fibroids are single nodules or clusters made up of muscle and connective tissue that grow in and on the uterus. According to the Cleveland Clinic, 40 to 80 percent of women have fibroids that do not cause any symptoms because they are typically small fibroids. However, large fibroids can result in a variety of uncomfortable symptoms, including excessive or painful bleeding during menstruation, bleeding between periods, bloating, pain during sex, and frequent urination. Treatment can range from over-the-counter pain medication to hormonal birth control and hormone-releasing sprays and injections, oral therapies, and a variety of surgeries.[11]

Adenomyosis is a condition in which the tissue that normally lines the uterus grows into the muscular wall of the uterus. This can result in an enlarged uterus, severe cramping, chronic pelvic pain, painful intercourse, and heavy menstrual periods. According to the Mayo Clinic, adenomyosis is most prevalent in women in their forties and fifties. Treatment may include anti-inflammatory drugs, including over-the-counter medications; hormone medications; or a hysterectomy.[12]

HYSTERECTOMIES

A hysterectomy is the surgical removal of the uterus. As such, people who have a hysterectomy will not be able to conceive. There are different types of hysterectomies, depending on the reason for surgery. These can range from removal of the uterus and cervix to removal of the uterus, cervix, fallopian tubes, ovaries, and upper portion of the vagina, as well as some tissue and lymph nodes. A hysterectomy can be used to treat endometriosis, uterine fibroids, and adenomyosis, as well as gynecological cancers. A hysterectomy may also be a form of gender-affirming care for transgender men.

Chapter Five: Reproductive Health

Pregnancy

Fertilization occurs when sperm and egg join together. From intercourse, this fertilization takes place when the sperm travels from the vagina through the cervix and uterus. After ejaculation, the sperm enters the fallopian tubes where an egg is capable of being fertilized if this occurs during the ovulation period. The fertilized egg descends to the uterus, and after approximately five to six days, implantation in the uterus occurs.[13] The following section on pregnancy options discusses other procedures, including egg fertilization, sperm donation, in vitro fertilization, and intrauterine insemination, as alternatives to fertilization through intercourse.

Often the first symptoms of pregnancy are a missed menstrual period, tender and swollen breasts, nausea, increased urination, and fatigue. However, other signs may include light spotting, cramps, bloating, constipation, and nasal congestion.[14] Pregnancy timing is based on gestational age, or how far along someone is in their pregnancy. A typical pregnancy ranges from thirty-eight to forty-two weeks. Delivery that occurs before thirty-seven weeks is considered premature. These weeks are broken into trimesters, or stages of pregnancy: first trimester (zero to thirteen weeks), second trimester (fourteen to twenty-six weeks), and third trimester (twenty-seven to forty weeks).[15] In these stages, the pregnant person's body changes. People may come to the library looking for information about the changes going on within their own bodies. People may also come to the library looking for information and resources about how they can conceive and prepare for pregnancy.

PREGNANCY COMPLICATIONS: ECTOPIC PREGNANCY AND PREECLAMPSIA

As previously noted, implantation occurs in the uterus about five to six days after an egg is fertilized. Sometimes the fertilized egg implants and grows outside of the main cavity of the uterus. This is called an ectopic pregnancy and happens in about one out of fifty pregnancies.*

Part II: Education

> In an ectopic pregnancy, implantation may occur in a fallopian tube, an ovary, the abdominal cavity, or the cervix. Ectopic pregnancies cannot proceed normally. The longer that an ectopic pregnancy is left untreated, the greater the risk of a rupture that can lead to life-threatening bleeding. Treatment may include medicinal or surgical removal of the fetus.[†]
>
> Preeclampsia is a medical condition that can occur about halfway through a pregnancy. People with preeclampsia experience high blood pressure, swelling, headaches, and blurred vision. According to the Cleveland Clinic, preeclampsia is the cause of about 15 percent of premature deliveries. Eclampsia can lead to seizures, coma, and death. Postpartum eclampsia is when someone develops preeclampsia after their baby is born. The earlier that it is detected, the better that it can be treated and managed with a health care provider.[‡]
>
> When selecting pregnancy material, be sure to include resources that have information about pregnancy complications and consider partnering with health organizations to discuss the stages and experiences of pregnancy.
>
> *"Complications of Pregnancy," Johns Hopkins Medicine, www.hopkinsmedicine.org/health/conditions-and-diseases/staying-healthy-during-pregnancy/complications-of-pregnancy.
>
> †"Ectopic Pregnancy—Symptoms and Causes," Mayo Clinic, March 12, 2022, www.mayoclinic.org/diseases-conditions/ectopic-pregnancy/symptoms-causes/syc-20372088#:%7E:text=An%20ectopic%20pregnancy%20occurs%20when,is%20called%20a%20tubal%20pregnancy.
>
> ‡"Preeclampsia: Symptoms, Causes, Treatments and Prevention," Cleveland Clinic, https://my.clevelandclinic.org/health/diseases/17952-preeclampsia.

Fertility, Infertility, and Pregnancy Options

Fertility is a person's ability to get pregnant. According to the American College of Obstetricians and Gynecologists, a woman's peak reproductive years are between the late teens and the late twenties. Fertility rapidly declines by a woman's midthirties, and conceiving naturally becomes very unlikely by age forty-five. Older women are more likely to experience issues that may affect fertility, such as uterine fibroids and endometriosis.[16]

Infertility is the inability to get pregnant despite frequent, unprotected sex for at least one year. Infertility is not uncommon. In fact, the Mayo Clinic estimates that 10 to 15 percent of couples are infertile. As such, they may seek information about fertility or to better understand infertility.[17] Infertility can be caused by a variety of factors, including disruption of testicular, ejaculatory, or ovarian functions; hormonal disorders; genetic disorders; fallopian tube obstruction; or other reproductive health issues. For example, PCOS may cause someone to not ovulate or to ovulate irregularly.[18]

Furthermore, doctors can formally diagnose someone as infertile through the results of several tests, including, but not limited to, pelvic exam, blood test, transvaginal ultrasound, scrotal ultrasound, semen analysis, and hysteroscopy. Treatments may include fertility drugs and surgical procedures.[19] For example, people may also try one of these options to become pregnant:

intrauterine insemination (IUI): an insemination procedure in which a doctor places sperm directly into the uterus to fertilize the egg

in vitro fertilization (IVF): a fertilization procedure that includes the sperm fertilizing eggs in a lab dish, with one of the embryos placed in the uterus or frozen for later

intracytoplasmic sperm injection (ICSI): a procedure that injects sperm directly into an egg before transferring an embryo into the uterus

egg fertilization/donation, sperm donation, and surrogacy: alternative options that involve a third party donating eggs, sperm, or embryos or using a surrogate to carry the pregnancy and give birth

The World Health Organization (WHO) asserts that diagnosis and treatment of infertility are "often not prioritized in national population and development policies and reproductive health strategies and are rarely covered through public health financing."[20] WHO contends that discussion of infertility should be incorporated in sex education programs and in sexual health discussions, resources, and materials.[21]

BIRTHING OPTIONS AND EXPERIENCES

Different types of birthing methods include vaginal delivery, assisted vaginal delivery, Cesarean delivery, and vaginal birth after Cesarean. Additionally, some people may want to have an at-home birth, a water birth, or a hospital birth. People can work with health care providers to develop a birth plan to describe their preferences for labor and delivery. As such, the library may want to provide resources that will help people learn about birthing methods and options and how to develop birth plans in consultation with a provider.*

It is also worthwhile for libraries to provide information and resources about postpartum depression (PPD) and postpartum psychosis, which are emotional and mental health conditions that can manifest after pregnancy and childbirth. The library can help provide resources and educational programs that destigmatize the very real and complicated experiences of being a parent.

*"Pregnancy: Types of Delivery," Cleveland Clinic, last reviewed October 7, 2022, https://my.clevelandclinic.org/health/articles/9675-pregnancy-types-of-delivery.

Pregnancy Loss

Miscarriage is the spontaneous loss of a pregnancy before the twentieth week of gestation. About 10 to 20 percent of pregnancies end in miscarriage. However, medical experts estimate that the number may be even higher as many miscarriages occur so early in pregnancy that people may not even know that they are pregnant.[22] Miscarriages that occur naturally are sometimes called spontaneous abortions by medical professionals. Signs of a miscarriage may include vaginal bleeding or spotting, pain or cramping in the lower abdomen or back, and fluid or tissue passing from the vagina. Options to treat the miscarriage, in consultation with a medical professional, may include letting the miscarriage progress naturally or receiving medical or surgical treatment to remove tissue.[23]

The Cleveland Clinic defines a stillbirth as when a fetus unexpectedly dies between the twentieth and thirty-sixth week of pregnancy. Stillbirths occur in about one out of 160 births in the United States. A medical professional will confirm via ultrasound whether the fetus has died. Depending on the situation, options for management, in consultation with a care provider, include inducing labor, natural birth, and Cesarean section. The cause of the stillbirth can be determined using a variety of tests, such as blood, genetic, and thyroid function, and through examination of the umbilical cord, membranes, and placenta.[24]

Pregnancy loss can be very emotional and cause grief, anger, sadness, and confusion. People may choose to see a therapist or counselor, arrange a funeral, and take time off from work or other commitments. As information professionals, we can provide resources related to not only the physical experience of pregnancy loss but also the emotional and mental aspects.

ADOPTION

When exploring pregnancy options, people may choose to put a child up for adoption after giving birth. Additionally, people may opt for adoption as an alternative to having their own biological children. Different types of adoption include open, closed, and semi-open. These options determine the type of communication and/or relationship that the birth parent and adoptive parents may form surrounding the adoption of the child. Resources about the adoption process from both the birth parent's and the adoptive parents' perspectives can be useful additions to the collection. Also consider adding resources about how to talk to children about being adopted, as well as material for teenagers and adults who are curious about their adoptive history.

Abortion

Abortion is a medical procedure to end a pregnancy. Studies have found that one in four women will have an abortion before she is forty-five years old. This number does not include trans, nonbinary, and gender-nonconforming people who also receive abortions.[25] Research has found that people get abortions for a variety of personal reasons, including financial, timing, partner-related, and health-related issues.[26]

The two main procedures for ending a pregnancy are a medical abortion or a surgical abortion. Medical abortions occur when the individual uses medication to terminate the pregnancy. This approach is most prevalent during the first trimester. A surgical abortion, sometimes called an in-clinic or aspiration procedure, removes the fetus and placenta from the uterus.[27] And while you may have seen billboards or social media posts offering abortion reversal procedures, there are presently no safe and effective options. In fact, the American College of Obstetricians and Gynecologists has described claims about abortion reversal treatments as "not based on science and do not meet clinical standards."[28]

The Centers for Disease Control and Prevention found that 93 percent of abortions occur within the first trimester.[29] Abortions after twenty-one weeks of gestation are very uncommon and account for less than 1 percent of all abortions in the United States. At this stage in pregnancy, an abortion procedure is very costly, is performed by only specialist abortion providers, and may take several days of treatment. Reasons for seeking an abortion at this stage vary. Some reasons might include medical concerns like major pregnancy complications or life endangerment of the pregnant person.[30]

ABORTION AND THE LAW

On June 24, 2022, the US Supreme Court overturned *Roe v. Wade*, repealing the constitutional right to abortion in effect since 1973. States are charged with determining the legality of abortion and under which circumstances, including trimester restrictions, appointment requirements, information provided for informed consent, and cost. As of this writing, twenty-six states are slated to ban abortion to the furthest extent possible. You can learn about your state's legal standing with regard to abortion on the Guttmacher Institute website (https://states.guttmacher.org/policies/).

Major medical bodies in the United States have declared their support for abortion and affirmed that abortion is health care and a component of comprehensive sexual and reproductive health services. These organizations include the American College of Obstetricians and Gynecologists, the American Medical Association, the American College of Physicians, and other medical associations.[31] Furthermore, human rights organizations, including the United Nations, have declared abortion to be a human right.[32]

Research has been conducted about the harms of denying abortion to people who seek this health care. The Turnaway Study is the first study to rigorously examine the effects of being denied a wanted abortion.[33] For five years, researchers interviewed nearly 1,000 women from thirty facilities around the United States who were denied a wanted abortion. Afterward, they compared their trajectories with women who did receive a wanted abortion. The findings revealed that denying abortion care significantly increases the odds of living in poverty, being unemployed, living without basic necessities, staying in abusive relationships, and developing serious health problems.

People may have a variety of feelings about abortion depending on their personal or religious convictions. This includes librarians who are reading this book and providing reference services. And although it is important to respect all opinions, it is also necessary to provide comprehensive information about sexual and reproductive health, including abortion care.

CRISIS PREGNANCY CENTERS

Crisis Pregnancy Centers are organizations that deter people from choosing an abortion. With more than 2,500 locations throughout the United States, they use misinformation and inaccurate health claims to dissuade people from making fully informed choices about how to proceed with their pregnancy.

A joint statement in the *Journal of Adolescent Health* by the Society of Adolescent Health and Medicine and the North American Society for Pediatric and Adolescent Gynecology explains how Crisis Pregnancy Centers lack medical and ethical practice standards.[*] Reasons include lack of staff with medical training or background, providing and promoting unproven services, prioritizing religious beliefs over client needs, and not promoting informed consent.

The *AMA Journal of Ethics* explains that Crisis Pregnancy Centers are legal because of freedom of speech, but that they are unethical and "do not meet the standard of patient-centered, quality medical care."[†] Furthermore, counseling provided at Crisis Pregnancy Centers falls "outside accepted medical standards and guidelines for providing evidence-based information and treatment options."[‡] When considering how you can develop partnerships with health organizations in the community, it is important that you work with legitimate health organizations that provide comprehensive, evidence-based information and services.

[*]Society for Adolescent Health and Medicine (SAHM) and the North American Society for Pediatric and Adolescent Gynecology (NASPAG), "Crisis Pregnancy Centers in the U.S.: Lack of Adherence to Medical and Ethical Practice Standards," *Journal of Adolescent Health* 65, no. 6 (2019): 821–824, https://doi.org/10.1016/j.jadohealth.2019.08.008.

[†]Amy G. Bryant, "Why Crisis Pregnancy Centers Are Legal but Unethical," *AMA Journal of Ethics*, March 1, 2018, https://journalofethics.ama-assn.org/article/why-crisis-pregnancy-centers-are-legal-unethical/2018-03.

[‡]SAHM and NASPAG, "Crisis Pregnancy Centers in the U.S."

Breast Health

In the United States, 264,000 cases of breast cancer are diagnosed in women and 2,400 cases of breast cancer are diagnosed in men. Breast cancer is a disease in which cells in the breast grow out of control. Symptoms may include new lumps in the breast or armpit; thickening or swelling; irritation of breast skin, including redness and flaky skin; pain in the nipple area and nipple discharge; change in breast size or shape; and overall pain.[34] Treatment options can include surgery, radiation therapy, chemotherapy, hormone therapy, targeted therapy, and immunotherapy.

Medical professionals recommend that people practice regular breast self-exams in order to get familiar with the makeup and feel of their breasts. This helps someone more readily notice any potentially harmful changes in their breast composition.[35] One of the most common procedures that doctors can do to detect breast cancer is a mammogram. Mammograms can be used to screen for potentially cancerous

Chapter Five: Reproductive Health

developments or to investigate any concerning changes in breasts. Mammograms are X-ray images, and the United States Preventive Services Task Force (USPSTF) recommends that women between fifty and seventy-four years old who are at average risk for breast cancer receive mammograms in two-year intervals.[36] Resources about how to prepare for a mammogram or how to do a breast self-exam can be valuable additions to your library collection. You may also consider providing programs that explain the mammogram process.

People may also seek surgery like breast augmentation and breast reduction procedures to change the appearance of their breasts. People may come to the library looking for information about breast surgery to suit personal preferences, breast reduction to ease chronic back pain and muscle spasms because of large breasts, or gender-affirming surgery. Information about breast health can include educational materials about understanding the makeup of breasts, breast diseases and prevention, and breast surgery.

BREASTFEEDING

Breastfeeding is a way to provide energy and nutrients to an infant through breast milk. WHO describes breast milk as the "ideal food for infants" as it contains important nutrients and antibodies that help protect against common childhood illnesses.[*] CDC reports that one in four infants are exclusively breastfed by the time they are six months old.[†]

However, many people are unable or choose not to breastfeed due to lactational complications, medical issues, and other conflicts, like work schedules and personal preferences. Infant formula is safe and nutritious and heavily regulated by the FDA. No parent should be made to feel guilty for choosing infant formula over breastfeeding.[‡]

Libraries can provide information about breastfeeding and breastfeeding alternatives. Additionally, the library should provide comfortable space for people to breastfeed, and staff should be trained to be respectful about people breastfeeding in the library. Library staff members who are pumping should be given the same courtesy and consideration. Currently, all fifty states and territories allow women to breastfeed in any public or private location.[§]

> *"Breastfeeding," World Health Organization, www.who.int/health-topics/breast feeding#tab=tab_1.
>
> †"Why It Matters," Centers for Disease Control and Prevention, last reviewed August 3, 2022, www.cdc.gov/breastfeeding/about-breastfeeding/why-it-matters.html.
>
> ‡Natasha Burgert, "Dear Pediatrician: Is It Okay If I Don't Breastfeed?," *Forbes*, updated July 20, 2022, www.forbes.com/health/family/unable-to-breastfeed/#:%7E:text=If%20you're%20unable%20or,baby%20is%202%20months%20old.
>
> §"Breastfeeding State Laws," National Conference of State Legislatures, August 26, 2021, www.ncsl.org/research/health/breastfeeding-state-laws.aspx.

The Prostate

The prostate is a gland that helps make semen. According to CDC, thirteen out of 100 American men will get prostate cancer in their lifetime. The risk of getting prostate cancer increases with genetic risk factors and age. The USPSTF recommends that men between fifty-five and sixty-nine years old speak to their medical provider about being screened for prostate cancer with the PSA test. Depending on the situation, common treatments may include surgery, radiation therapy, or management.[37] Consider hosting experts to speak about prostate health, as well as providing books and resource links for continued education.

Other Cancers

Cancer is a concept that brings up a lot of fear and anxiety in people. However, education about cancer is key. Not only will people be better able to communicate about concerns to their health care provider, but they can feel empowered to participate fully in their treatment process.

Testicular and Penile Cancer

Testicles, or testes, are organs that make hormones and sperm. Some men may experience a reduction in hormone production with age, although others may be able to make sperm well into older age. Medical professionals encourage people to examine their testes regularly to check for lumps, redness, or pain. Any pain, swelling, or lumps should be checked by a doctor for testicular cancer. Testicular cancer is most prevalent between the ages of twenty and thirty-nine.[38] A physical exam, biopsy, and laboratory and imaging tests can help make these diagnoses. Treatment may include surgery, radiation, or chemotherapy.

Gynecologic Cancers

Gynecological cancers are named for the different places in which they begin. These include cervical, ovarian, uterine, vaginal, and vulvar cancer. And while symptoms may vary depending on the type of cancer, the most common symptoms include abnormal vaginal bleeding or discharge, feeling full too quickly, bloating, difficulty eating for ovarian cancer, pelvic pain or pressure for ovarian and uterine cancers, more urgent need to urinate with ovarian and vaginal cancers, and pain and changes in the vulva skin and color for vulvar cancer.[39]

Pap smears, or pap tests, look for cancer cell changes in the cervix. The CDC recommends pap testing beginning at age twenty-one. Pending normal results, medical experts recommend that patients resume testing every three to five years. Pap smears can be an unnerving experience, especially for the first time. Consider acquiring material that demystifies the pap smear experience.

Many gynecological cancers do not have standard screening tests for early detection. As such, it is important that people be aware of symptoms and warning signs so that they can seek medical guidance earlier. Libraries can facilitate the sharing of this important information by spreading awareness of these topics.

Final Thoughts

This chapter includes quite a lot of definitions, terms, and descriptions! And although we are not expected to be experts on any of these topics, a basic understanding of such issues and any accompanying legislation can make us better stewards of our libraries and communities. Having been introduced to these topics, we can now look at our existing collections and decide where we need improvements. Additionally, we can consider local partnerships and collaborations that we can build to provide educational resources. I hope that this chapter has left you inspired with some ways that you can improve reproductive health information in your library. Soon we will coalesce all of these chapters together with some clear library-related actions.

Let's Review

- Librarians can provide information about a myriad of reproductive health issues that will empower people to better understand their bodies and communicate with health care providers.
- Menstruation and abortion are part of comprehensive reproductive health care. Instead of treating them as outliers, we can incorporate these issues into the reproductive health information and services that we provide.
- Pregnancy is a complex topic and providing resources about various pregnancy options is necessary. However, resources shared and partnerships formed should be evidence-based.
- Reproductive health–related cancers can be demystified and offer opportunities for libraries to provide information resources and community partnerships.

Reflection Questions

1. How can you facilitate providing information and forming educational partnerships on reproductive health–related topics.
2. What types of resources and guides can you create or collect that will encourage people to speak with a medical provider?
3. How can your library create an environment that encourages people to seek information about reproductive health?

NOTES

1. "Reproductive Health: Aims and Scope," BioMed Central, https://reproductive-health-journal.biomedcentral.com/submission-guidelines/aims-and-scope.
2. Mary J. Minkin and Carol V. Wright, *The Yale Guide to Women's Reproductive Health: From Menarche to Menopause* (Yale University Press, 2003).

Chapter Five: Reproductive Health

3. "Amenorrhea—Symptoms and Causes," Mayo Clinic, February 18, 2021, www.mayoclinic.org/diseases-conditions/amenorrhea/symptoms-causes/syc-20369299#:%7E:text=Overview,a%20period%20by%20age%2015.
4. Giovanni Grandi et al., "Prevalence of Menstrual Pain in Young Women: What Is Dysmenorrhea?," *Journal of Pain Research* 5 (2012): 169–74, https://doi.org/10.2147/JPR.S30602.
5. "Dysmenorrhea: Painful Periods," ACOG, last updated December 2020, www.acog.org/womens-health/faqs/dysmenorrhea-painful-periods.
6. Chen X. Chen, Claire B. Draucker, and Janet S. Carpenter, "What Women Say about Their Dysmenorrhea: A Qualitative Thematic Analysis," *BMC Women's Health* 18, no. 47 (2018), https://doi.org/10.1186/s12905-018-0538-8.
7. "Menopause—Diagnosis and Treatment," Mayo Clinic, October 14, 2020, www.mayoclinic.org/diseases-conditions/menopause/diagnosis-treatment/drc-20353401.
8. "Perimenopause—Symptoms and Causes," Mayo Clinic, August 7, 2021, www.mayoclinic.org/diseases-conditions/perimenopause/symptoms-causes/syc-20354666#:%7E:text=Perimenopause%20means%20%22around%20menopause%22%20and,start%20perimenopause%20at%20different%20ages.
9. "Dysmenorrhea," Johns Hopkins Medicine, www.hopkinsmedicine.org/health/conditions-and-diseases/dysmenorrhea#:%7E:text=Secondary%20dysmenorrhea%20is%20caused%20by,%2C%20infection%2C%20and%20pelvic%20pain.
10. "Endometriosis," Office on Women's Health, last updated February 22, 2021, www.womenshealth.gov/a-z-topics/endometriosis#:%7E:text=Endometriosis%20is%20a%20common%20health,the%20United%20States%2C%20have%20endometriosis.
11. "Uterine Fibroids: Symptoms, Causes, Risk Factors and Treatment," Cleveland Clinic, last reviewed August 24, 2020, https://my.clevelandclinic.org/health/diseases/9130-uterine-fibroids.
12. "Adenomyosis—Diagnosis and Treatment," Mayo Clinic, June 18, 2022, www.mayoclinic.org/diseases-conditions/adenomyosis/diagnosis-treatment/drc-20369143.
13. "Conception: How It Works," UCSF Health, www.ucsfhealth.org/education/conception-how-it-works.
14. "Symptoms of Pregnancy: What Happens First," Mayo Clinic, December 3, 2021, www.mayoclinic.org/healthy-lifestyle/getting-pregnant/in-depth/symptoms-of-pregnancy/art-20043853?reDate=25072022.

Part II: Education

15. "Pregnancy: The Three Trimesters," UCSF Health, www.ucsfhealth.org/conditions/pregnancy/trimesters.
16. "Having a Baby After Age 35: How Aging Affects Fertility and Pregnancy," ACOG, last reviewed December 2021, www.acog.org/womens-health/faqs/having-a-baby-after-age-35-how-aging-affects-fertility-and-pregnancy.
17. "Infertility—Symptoms and Causes," Mayo Clinic, September 1, 2021, www.mayoclinic.org/diseases-conditions/infertility/symptoms-causes/syc-20354317.
18. "Infertility," Centers for Disease Control and Prevention, last reviewed March 1, 2022, www.cdc.gov/reproductivehealth/infertility/index.htm.
19. "Infertility Causes: Types, Risk Factors, Diagnosis and Treatment," Cleveland Clinic, last reviewed December 13, 2020, https://my.clevelandclinic.org/health/diseases/16083-infertility-causes.
20. "Infertility," World Health Organization (WHO), September 14, 2020, www.who.int/news-room/fact-sheets/detail/infertility.
21. "Infertility," WHO.
22. "Miscarriage—Diagnosis and Treatment," Mayo Clinic, October 16, 2021, www.mayoclinic.org/diseases-conditions/pregnancy-loss-miscarriage/diagnosis-treatment/drc-20354304.
23. "Miscarriage," MedlinePlus, National Library of Medicine, https://medlineplus.gov/ency/article/001488.htm#:%7E:text=Miscarriage%20is%20a%20naturally%20occurring,of%20conception%20leave%20the%20body.
24. "Stillbirth: Definition, Causes and Prevention," Cleveland Clinic, last reviewed August 27, 2020, https://my.clevelandclinic.org/health/diseases/9685-stillbirth.
25. "Abortion Is a Common Experience for U.S. Women, Despite Dramatic Declines in Rates," Guttmacher Institute, October 19, 2017, www.guttmacher.org/news-release/2017/abortion-common-experience-us-women-despite-dramatic-declines-rates.
26. M. Antonia Biggs, Heather Gould, and Diana Greene Foster, "Understanding Why Women Seek Abortions in the US," *BMC Women's Health* 13, no. 29 (2013), https://doi.org/10.1186/1472-6874-13-29.
27. "Abortion," MedlinePlus, National Library of Medicine, last updated August 5, 2022, https://medlineplus.gov/abortion.html.
28. "Medication Abortion Reversal Is Not Supported by Science," ACOG (American College of Obstetricians and Gynecologists), www.acog.org/advocacy/facts-are-important/medication-abortion-reversal-is-not-supported-by-science.

29. Jeff Diamant, and Besheer Mohamed, "What the Data Says about Abortion in the U.S.," Pew Research Center, June 24, 2022, www.pewresearch.org/fact-tank/2022/06/24/what-the-data-says-about-abortion-in-the-u-s-2/#:%7E:text=The%20vast%20majority%20of%20abortions,gestation%2C%20according%20to%20the%20CDC.
30. "CDCs Abortion Surveillance System FAQs," Centers for Disease Control and Prevention, last reviewed November 22, 2021, www.cdc.gov/reproductivehealth/data_stats/abortion.htm.
31. Janice Hopkins Tanne, "Roe v Wade: Medical Bodies Declare Support for Abortion Rights, as Doctors and States Face Confusion," *The BMJ*, July 4, 2022, www.bmj.com/content/378/bmj.o1643.
32. "Access to Safe and Legal Abortion: Urgent Call for United States to Adhere to Women's Rights Convention, UN Committee," OHCHR (Office for the High Commissioner of Human Rights), July 1, 2022, www.ohchr.org/en/statements/2022/07/access-safe-and-legal-abortion-urgent-call-united-states-adhere-womens-rights.
33. Diana Greene Foster, *The Turnaway Study: Ten Years, a Thousand Women, and the Consequences of Having—or Being Denied—an Abortion.* New York: Scribner, 2021.
34. "Basic Information about Breast Cancer," Centers for Disease Control and Prevention, last reviewed September 26, 2022, www.cdc.gov/cancer/breast/basic_info/.
35. "Breast Anatomy: Breast Cancer, Breastfeeding, Conditions," Cleveland Clinic, last reviewed October 14, 2020, https://my.clevelandclinic.org/health/articles/8330-breast-anatomy.
36. "What Is Breast Cancer Screening?," Centers for Disease Control and Prevention, last reviewed September 26, 2022, www.cdc.gov/cancer/breast/basic_info/screening.htm#:%7E:text=The%20USPSTF%20recommends%20that%20women,often%20to%20get%20a%20mammogram.
37. "Basic Information about Prostate Cancer," Centers for Disease Control and Prevention, last reviewed August 25, 2022, www.cdc.gov/cancer/prostate/basic_info/.
38. "Testicular Cancer," MedlinePlus, National Library of Medicine, last updated April 10, 2018, https://medlineplus.gov/testicularcancer.html.
39. "Basic Information about Gynecologic Cancers," Centers for Disease Control and Prevention, last reviewed August 30, 2022, www.cdc.gov/cancer/gynecologic/basic_info/.

CHAPTER SIX

LGBTQIA+ Sexual and Reproductive Health Topics

PREVIOUS CHAPTERS HAVE dived into such topics like pap smears, birth control, STI prevention, and so on. All of those are applicable to LGBTQIA+ individuals. However, members of the LGBTQIA+ community may have some specific needs related to their sexual and reproductive health. The purpose of this chapter is to provide context for these important SRH needs of the LGBTQIA+ community.

Overview of Health Care and the LGBTQIA+ Community

Before we dive into LGBTQIA+ specific topics, it is important for us to understand the very real historic and contemporary barriers that people in this community have faced related to their health care.

Pathologization

To begin with, LGBTQIA+ people have historically been treated as if they were mentally ill. In fact, the first edition of the *Diagnostic and Statistical Manual of Mental Disorders (DSM-1),* which is used by clinicians and researchers to diagnose and classify mental disorders, classified homosexuality as a "sociopathic personality disturbance." In the second edition in 1968, it reclassified it as a "sexual deviation."[1] This meant that LGBTQIA+ folks were subjected to dangerous and degrading treatments in attempts to change them. This classification was removed in 1973 thanks to LGBTQIA+ activists who raised awareness, mobilized, and spoke at the annual American Psychiatric Association conference in May 1973.[2]

Until 2013, gender identity disorder was listed in the *DSM*. This diagnosis was used to pathologize transgender individuals as mentally ill. It was replaced with gender dysphoria, which is used to describe emotional distress over "a marked incongruence between one's experienced/expressed gender and assigned gender."[3] Many trans rights activists do not believe that gender dysphoria should be included in the *DSM* as it still pathologizes LGBTQIA+ people and can be weaponized against them in some insurance coverage.[4]

Another example of the continued pathologization of the LGBTQIA+ community exists in diagnoses of asexual people. Asexual people may be diagnosed by medical professionals with a mood disorder or hormonal imbalance. Patients may be prescribed medication to treat low sex drive. In a piece about of asexuality, Michele Kirichanskaya explains that "when many asexuals disclose their identity, doctors attempt to 'treat' their asexuality like it's a medical issue instead of a legitimate identity of which they claim ownership."[5]

Conversion Therapy

Conversion therapy is a discredited and dangerous practice that is still legal in most of the United States. Conversion therapy—or reparative therapy—seeks to change the sexual orientation, gender identity, or gender expression of an individual. Through harmful and damaging practices, LGBTQIA+ people, particularly youth, are subjected to "treatments" in order to "cure" them. Not only are these practices degrading and ineffective, but they also leave people who have experienced conversion therapy with a greater risk for depression, anxiety, and self-destructive behavior, such as drug misuse and suicide.[6] Research has found that 698,000 LGBTQIA+ adults between the ages of eighteen and fifty-nine in the United States have undergone conversion therapy. This includes 350,000 adults who received treatment as adolescents.[7]

These practices have been condemned by every major medical and mental health organization for decades.[8] And yet only twenty states and the District of Columbia have laws that fully protect minors from

Chapter Six: LGBTQIA+ Sexual and Reproductive Health Topics

conversion therapy. In states where there aren't full protections against conversion therapy, there may be local ordinances and protections. However, much work needs to be done to end conversion therapy practices.[9] Consider educating your library patrons through programs and resources about the dangers of conversion therapy. You may also want to look into state and county legislation to see if conversion therapy has been banned in your library's community.

> ### INTRO TO INTERSEX
>
> *Intersex* individuals are people who have a chromosome combination that doesn't match the binary categories of XX and XY chromosomes. Intersex individuals make up nearly 2 percent of the population and may have a variety of differences in genitalia, internal sex organs, hormone production, hormone response, and/or secondary sex traits. Historically, intersex babies and children have been subjected to surgical procedures to change genital appearance or to reposition or remove reproductive organs. As such, people born intersex may grow up not connecting with the gender that they were assigned via surgery. They may be diagnosed with gender dysphoria and depression. Intersex individuals do not always identify as LGBTQ+, but they often face social stigma and discrimination that is rooted in homophobia, biphobia, and transphobia.* Learn more on the website of interACT: Advocates for Intersex Youth (https://interactadvocates.org).
>
> *"Understanding the Intersex Community," Human Rights Campaign, www.hrc.org/resources/understanding-the-intersex-community.

The Health Care System

Because of historical and contemporary discrimination and stigma, LGBTQIA+ people may avoid the health care system completely. In fact, research has found that almost 25 percent of transgender patients in the United States delay seeking treatment because of concerns of mistreatment.[10] According to research by the Kaiser Family Foundation, LGBTQIA+ individuals are more likely to report that providers do not believe them, blame them for their health problems, assume something about them, or dismiss their concerns.[11]

Although the Biden administration restored a policy established by the Obama administration that protects LGBTQIA+ people under the federal health care discrimination provision, only 41 percent of the LGBTQIA+ population lives in a state with insurance protections that include sexual orientation and gender identity.[12] One in four LGBTQIA+ people reported that their preferred provider was not included in their health insurance coverage. Since LGBTQIA+ adults are twice as likely as the general population to have experienced homelessness in their lifetimes, they face higher medical bills as well as barriers to paying for health care and receiving the affirming care that they deserve.[13]

As such, LGBTQIA+ women have reported lower rates of accessing gynecological exams and reproductive health services like cervical and breast cancer screening, education, and counseling. The Kaiser Family Foundation found that 20 percent of lesbian women and 12 percent of bisexual women between the ages of eighteen and sixty-four in the United States have never seen a doctor or a nurse for a gynecological exam. In terms of contraception, LGBTQIA+ people have higher rates of using contraception to manage a medical condition than non-LGBTQIA+ people. The report further found that bisexual women have more concerns about unwanted pregnancy than non-LGBTQIA+ people and are less confident in their contraceptive methods.[14]

This information is important for public libraries. We can develop partnerships with inclusive health organizations that can educate patrons on their options. We can also develop resource guides specific to LGBTQIA+ health concerns and needs.

Court Cases and Legislation

There have been—and continue to be—major legislative barriers to comprehensive LGBTQIA+ health care. An understanding of these laws is important to determine how we can provide and present information to our communities.

In 1996 the Defense of Marriage Act (DOMA) was a federal law that defined marriage as a union between a man and a woman. It also allowed states to not recognize same-sex marriages that were performed and recognized under other state laws. This meant that same-sex couples were long denied over 1,000 federal protections and privileges, including their rights to visitation and medical decision making for their partners.[15]

In 2011 new regulations went into effect when the Obama administration created guidelines that were issued to the Department of Health and Human Services. Nevertheless, some hospitals still issued their own guidelines, removing or excluding partners from hospital rooms. DOMA was overturned in 2013, and this provided same-sex couples with the same federal benefits, like accessing employer-provided health insurance, receiving benefits, and filing jointly on taxes, as heterosexual couples. The Supreme Court legalized same-sex marriage in 2015 in *Obergefell v. Hodges*. At the time, thirteen states still banned same-sex marriage.[16]

Up until 2003 nonprocreative sex, or antisodomy, laws were still in effect in the United States. In 1982 Michael Hardwick was charged with violating a Georgia statute for engaging in consensual intercourse with a man.[17] Hardwick challenged the constitutionality of the law, but it wasn't until 2003 in *Lawrence v. Texas* that the Supreme Court ruled that nonprocreative sex laws violated one's privacy. Thirteen active laws were overturned.[18]

In 2014 the US Department of Education issued guidelines that stated that Title IX, a civil rights law that prohibits sex discrimination in education, also protects trans students. As such, trans students would be able to use the bathrooms and locker rooms that correspond with their gender identities. However, in 2018 the Trump administration revoked this. In June 2021 this revocation was reversed, and the US Department of Education's Office for Civil Rights explained that Title IX's prohibition on discrimination on the basis of sex included protection from discrimination based on sexual orientation and gender identity.[19]

This is important because statistics from the CDC detail the high rates of violence that LGBTQIA+ youth experience at school. In a 2015 national survey, 34 percent of respondents reported that they had been bullied at school, 23 percent had experienced sexual dating violence in the twelve months before the survey was conducted, and 18 percent had been forced to have sexual intercourse at some point in their lives.[20]

Part II: Education

Transition

As explained, the information in the previous chapters is intended to be inclusive of LGBTQIA+ communities. However, there are also unique aspects that deserve their own sections. Transition is one of these sections.

When a person's gender identity does not align with their physical body, they may transition. Each transition is personal and looks different for every individual. This process may include social, medical, and legal components. The social transition is when one starts to adjust their dress and demeanor, such as their clothing, hairstyle, voice, and mannerisms, to reflect their gender identity. It may also include telling people one's chosen name and pronouns. The legal transition involves updating name and gender on official documents, school and state records, licenses, birth certificates, Social Security cards, and passports. Medical transition occurs when one undergoes physical procedures to change their physical body. Methods can include hormone blockers, hormone replacement therapy, and gender confirmation surgery. To be clear, one's identity is not dependent on transition or procedures. While some people may want their identities to be recognized without undergoing medical procedures, others simply may not have access to the necessary medical care.[21]

The World Professional Association for Transgender Health (WPATH) has created a standards-of-care document for those going through medical transition. This document outlines "evidence-based care, education, research, advocacy, public policy, and respect in transsexual and transgender health."[22] The standards include guidelines for mental health professionals to discuss gender identity, gender expression, and options. Before surgeries or hormonal treatments, individuals are expected to significantly transition into their gender identities.

Hormone therapy (HT) is the process of putting sex hormones that reflects one's gender identity into one's body. These hormones may also suppress or reduce hormones that one's body naturally makes. This therapy may involve injections, pills, or topical solutions, depending on the procedure. For example, FTM (female-to-male) trans people can be given hormones that help develop muscles and body hair while suppressing and ending menstruation. For MTF (male-to-female) trans people, hormones can change muscle matter, fat distribution, and reduce body hair.[23]

Gender confirmation surgery (GCS), also known as gender affirmation surgery, is the process of undergoing physical surgeries to reflect one's gender identity. (Note: Avoid terms like *pre-op, post-op, sex change,* and *gender reassignment* as they stigmatize this process.) For MTF trans people, GCS may include, but is not limited to, top surgeries like breast enlargement and plastic surgery and facial feminization surgeries and bottom surgeries such as genital reconstruction and penile skin inversion vaginoplasty.[24] For FTM trans people, surgeries may include, but are not limited to, top surgeries such as removing breasts, and facial masculinization surgeries and bottom surgeries like hysterectomy, metoidioplasty, and phalloplasty to form a penis and urethra.[25]

The transition process can be an exciting, affirming, confusing, and/or lonely experience. Libraries should provide books and resources that not only demystify the transition process but also discuss the emotional aspects. Materials about how to communicate their transition to others, including medical professionals, are important. It is also necessary to include information for family and friends to learn about how they can support someone in their transition.

Pregnancy and Contraception

Sexual and reproductive health information is often described as women's or men's health services. However, this information is pertinent to people of all different identities so libraries should use language and develop collections that are inclusive.

Pregnancy

In addition to pregnancy options discussed previously, here are some more concepts that LGBTQIA+ people may wish to utilize.[26] This information can be provided in the library's collection and online resources.

> **sperm donation:** Depending on the situation, people may wish to work with either a known donor or a sperm bank donor. People may also do at-home insemination or have an intrauterine

insemination (IUI) procedure with a doctor. If the IUI is unsuccessful, people may opt for in vitro fertilization (IVF).

egg fertilization/donation: Reciprocal IVF, also known as partner-assisted reproduction, is when one partner's eggs are retrieved and fertilized with donor sperm and the embryo is transferred to the uterus of the other partner. LGBTQIA+ people may also seek egg donations from someone, fertilizing the egg with sperm either from a partner or from a donor, and transferring it to either a genetic or surrogate carrier.

surrogacy: This option includes working with someone to carry the pregnancy. Surrogacy can be either traditional or gestational. Traditional is when the pregnant person is the genetic parent whereas gestational surrogacy is when the person carrying the pregnancy is not genetically related.

egg freezing and embryo creation: Trans men who want genetically related families in the future may consider freezing their eggs or embryos before or early on in HT. This gives trans men the option of carrying the pregnancy themselves, giving their eggs to a partner through reciprocal IVF, or working with a gestational surrogate.

sperm freezing: Transgender women may freeze sperm for later insemination. Transgender men who retain their ovaries and uterus may still be able to get pregnant.

An important note is that a qualitative study found that pregnant transgender people experienced transphobia, inappropriate medical care, and institutional erasure. Notably, some respondents explained how they decided to pass as cisgender women so that they would avoid judgment, discrimination, or even violence. One participant explained, "[I was] intentionally trying to be inconspicuous and fly below the radar. I wanted to be able to present as male, but I made that decision [to present as female] at that time because I was afraid."[27] As such, library books, resources, programs, and partnerships surrounding pregnancy and fertility should be inclusive of different identities without making assumptions about anybody seeking the information.

Contraception

In terms of preventing pregnancy, there is much terrain for libraries to cover. To begin with, research published in the *American Journal of Public Health* found that adult cisgender sexual minority women (queer, bisexual, lesbian, pansexual) have an elevated risk of unintended pregnancy.[28] Participants explained that they have faced barriers to preventing unwanted pregnancy. These include feeling excluded from conversations about contraception, shame of navigating their own identities and appropriate contraception, experiencing sexual assault, and ignorance by health care professionals about their identities and pregnancy prevention. However, the study also found that participants wanted queer-positive, sex-positive contraception. As one participant explained, "It wasn't until I came out as non-straight that I had enough of a hold on my identity and a grasp on feminism and health. And I think that's when my negotiation [in sexual relationships] shifted for the better."[29] Libraries can harness this information to provide resources about contraception that go beyond the binary.

Studies have also found that pregnancy prevention is an important topic of discussion for LGBTQIA+ youth. A study by the American Academy of Pediatrics found that bisexual teens had nearly five times the risk of teen pregnancy.[30] Those who identified as mostly heterosexual or lesbian had two times the risk of teen pregnancy. Research found that this may be because "sexual minority women who have been abused, bullied . . . may have sex with men as they grapple with feelings of depression, anxiety, low self-esteem or a desire to hide their sexuality."[31]

Therefore, it is imperative that libraries provide a safe, bully-free space where SRH information does not strictly focus on the heterosexual experience. Since a dramatically low number of LGBT students between the ages of thirteen and twenty-one reported that their health classes included positive representations of LGBT-related topics, libraries have an urgent need to fill.[32]

Part II: Education

CONTRACEPTION OPTIONS FOR THE LGBTQIA+ COMMUNITY

In addition to the contraception methods discussed previously, the following options are also important when providing comprehensive sexual and reproductive health information.

- Hormonal birth control can not only prevent pregnancy but also help regulate one's periods or temporarily halt them. This can be useful for people who still have monthly periods and do not want them.
- Progestogen-only pills prevent pregnancy and do not include estrogen.
- Contraceptives like external and internal condoms can prevent both pregnancy and STIs. Some people may consider a hysterectomy, tubal ligation, or vasectomy as more permanent options.

WPATH offers a provider search directory on its website (www.wpath.org/provider/search). Additionally, the GLMA: Health Professionals Advancing LGBTQ Equality provides information for both health care providers and patients on its website (www.glma.org).

Supporting the LGBTQIA+ Community

In addition to destigmatizing language surrounding sexual and reproductive health, it can be important to provide space and resources for LGBTQIA+ support groups. This could include connecting with a local student or community alliance, hosting a monthly LGBTQIA+ book club or discussion space, and partnering with health professionals who can provide educational information and presentations.

You may also want to consider forming a facilitated group for parents and caregivers of LGBTQIA+ children. Research has shown that LGBTQIA+ youth thrive when they grow up in a supportive, nonjudgmental, and safe environment. This group can help caregivers learn how they can create and foster those environments. Additionally, library materials should include resources for parents and caregivers so that they can self-educate.

Final Thoughts

Members of the LGBTQIA+ community experience many of the same sexual and reproductive health needs as cisgender and heterosexual individuals. The LGBTQIA+ community may also have unique health needs. However, LGBTQIA+ folks face many medical barriers and social stigma. When the library focuses on inclusive SRH information, this may help LGBTQIA+ individuals better communicate their specific needs to health care professionals and find health care settings that are most aligned with their specific health goals.

Let's Review

- The LGBTQIA+ community has faced decades of pathologization whereby they have been treated as mentally ill or as second-class citizens. Stigma, erasure, ignorance, and transphobia in educational and medical spheres can hinder health care.
- Hormone therapy and gender confirmation surgery are two medical interventions that transgender people may complete to fully embrace their gender identities. However, medical procedures are not required for someone to identify as transgender.
- People of all gender identities and sexual orientations can get pregnant. Our resources should use inclusive language to represent the spectrum of people who may be pregnant.
- Public libraries must provide a space that not only affirms humanity but also empowers people to learn, communicate, and advocate for their health.

Reflection Questions

1. What resources can you add to your physical and digital collections for people who are contemplating transition? What about resources for people who decide to transition?
2. How can you provide pregnancy and contraception information and resources in an inclusive way?
3. What types of resources and partnerships can you tap into in your community to help build supportive networks for LGBTQIA+ patrons?

Part II: Education

NOTES

1. Jack Drescher, "Out of DSM: Depathologizing Homosexuality," *Behavioral Sciences* 5, no. 4 (2015): 565–75. doi:10.3390/bs5040565.
2. Ray Levy Uyeda, "How LGBTQ+ Activists Got 'Homosexuality' out of the DSM," *JSTOR Daily*, May 26, 2021, https://daily.jstor.org/how-lgbtq-activists-got-homosexuality-out-of-the-dsm/.
3. Dani Heffernan, "The APA Removes 'Gender Identity Disorder' from Updated Mental Health Guide," GLAAD, December 3, 2012, www.glaad.org/blog/apa-removes-gender-identity-disorder-updated-mental-health-guide.
4. Kayley Whalen, "(In)validating Transgender Identities: Progress and Trouble in the DSM-5," National LGBTQ Task Force, www.thetaskforce.org/invalidating-transgender-identities-progress-and-trouble-in-the-dsm-5/.
5. Michele Kirichanskaya, "Asexual People Aren't Broken. Doctors Still Treat Them as If They Are," Bitch Media, June 10, 2021, www.bitchmedia.org/article/doctors-still-mistreat-asexual-patients.
6. "Conversion Therapy," NAMI: National Alliance on Mental Illness, www.nami.org/Advocacy/Policy-Priorities/Stopping-Harmful-Practices/Conversion-Therapy.
7. "Conversion Therapy," GLAAD, November 8, 2018, www.glaad.org/conversiontherapy.
8. "The Lies and Dangers of Efforts to Change Sexual Orientation or Gender Identity," Human Rights Campaign, www.hrc.org/resources/the-lies-and-dangers-of-reparative-therapy.
9. "Ending Conversion Therapy," The Trevor Project, www.thetrevorproject.org/ending-conversion-therapy/.
10. Sandy E. James et al., *Executive Summary of the Report of the 2015 U.S. Transgender Survey* (Washington, DC: National Center for Transgender Equality, 2016).
11. Lindsey Dawson et al., "LGBT+ People's Health and Experiences Accessing Care—Report," KFF, July 22, 2021, www.kff.org/report-section/lgbt-peoples-health-and-experiences-accessing-care-report/.
12. "Healthcare Laws and Policies," Movement Advancement Project, as of October 13, 2022, www.lgbtmap.org/equality-maps/healthcare_laws_and_policies.
13. Bianca D. M. Wilson et al., "Homelessness Among LGBT Adults in the US," Williams Institute, May 2020, https://williamsinstitute.law.ucla.edu/publications/lgbt-homelessness-us/.

14. Kate Sosin, "'Don't Say Gay' Bills Aren't New. They've Just Been Revived," The 19th, April 20, 2022, https://19thnews.org/2022/04/dont-say-gay-existed-before-florida-alabama-laws/.
15. "Defense of Marriage Act (DOMA)." LII / Legal Information Institute, last updated September 2022, www.law.cornell.edu/wex/defense_of_marriage_act_(doma).
16. "*Obergefell v. Hodges*—A Brief History of Civil Rights in the United States,"HUSL Library at Howard University School of Law, https://library.law.howard.edu/civilrightshistory/lgbtq/obergefell.
17. *Bowers v. Hardwick*, Oyez, www.oyez.org/cases/1985/85-140.
18. *Lawrence v. Texas*, Oyez, www.oyez.org/cases/2002/02-102.
19. "U.S. Department of Education Confirms Title IX Protects Students from Discrimination Based on Sexual Orientation and Gender Identity," US Department of Education, June 16, 2021, www.ed.gov/news/press-releases/us-department-education-confirms-title-ix-protects-students-discrimination-based-sexual-orientation-and-gender-identity.
20. Dawson et al., "LGBT+ People's Health and Experiences Accessing Care."
21. Jo Langford, *The Pride Guide: A Guide to Sexual and Social Health for LGBTQ Youth* (Lanham, MD: Rowman & Littlefield, 2020).
22. Eli Coleman et al., "Standards of Care for the Health of Transgender and Gender Diverse People, Version 8," *International Journal of Transgender Health* 23, supp. 1 (2022), https://doi.org/10.1080/26895269.2022.2100644.
23. "Transgender Hormone Therapy: Getting Started," UVA Health, https://uvahealth.com/services/transgender/transgender-hormone-therapy.
24. "MTF Surgery for Trans Women," UVA Health, https://uvahealth.com/services/transgender/transgender-mtf-surgery.
25. "Female to Male Surgery for Trans Men," UVA Health, https://uvahealth.com/services/transgender/transgender-ftm-surgery.
26. Alex Vance, "Fertility Options for Transgender People," Verywell Family, June 24, 2021, www.verywellfamily.com/fertility-options-for-transgender-people-5186040.
27. Alexis Hoffkling, Juno Obedin-Maliver, and Jae Sevelius, "From Erasure to Opportunity: A Qualitative Study of the Experiences of Transgender Men around Pregnancy and Recommendations for Providers," *BMC Pregnancy Childbirth* 17, no. 332 (2017).

Part II: Education

28. Jenny A. Higgins et al., "Sexual Minority Women and Contraceptive Use: Complex Pathways between Sexual Orientation and Health Outcomes," *American Journal of Public Health* 109, no. 12 (December 2019): 1680–86.
29. Higgins et al., "Sexual Minority Women and Contraceptive Use."
30. Melissa Jenco, "Teen Pregnancy among Sexual Minorities Linked to Abuse: Study," American Academy of Pediatrics, March 12, 2018, https://publications.aap.org/aapnews/news/14269?autologincheck=redirected.
31. Jenco, "Teen Pregnancy among Sexual Minorities."
32. "American Adolescents' Sources of Sexual Health Information," Guttmacher Institute, December 2017, www.guttmacher.org/fact-sheet/facts-american-teens-sources-information-about-sex.

PART III

Implementation

Integrating sexual and reproductive health information isn't too dissimilar from providing any other type of library service or program. It is more a matter of taking these steps thoughtfully and intentionally. This means that we should be cognizant of the types of formats that we provide, ensure inclusive reference services, and develop meaningful partnerships that advance health. The rest of this book is about making this happen at your library, moving forward, and keeping abreast of current resources.

PART III

Implementation

CHAPTER SEVEN

Sexual and Reproductive Health at Your Library

THIS CHAPTER DISCUSSES how you can integrate SRH information into your collections, programming, reference services, and community partnerships. This is the opportunity to put what we have learned into practice. So let's continue on!

Anxiety and Bias in Public Library Services

I find it necessary to begin this chapter with a discussion of identity work and biases. Such discourse is foundational to considering how we can provide library services, programs, and collaborations.

Let's first discuss library anxiety. Library anxiety is a very real phenomenon that impacts how people utilize their libraries. *Library anxiety*, a term coined by Constance A. Mellon in 1986, refers to a fear of libraries and librarians and a sense of inadequacy in using the library.[1] Nearly forty years later, this remains a useful framework as scholars have noted that "the library's resources do not seem to be as friendly and intuitive as the commercial search engines that students are familiar with" and that "most people in all types of libraries suffer from confusion and uncertainty, especially with a difficult, complex information-seeking assignment."[2]

I see this firsthand in my own work as a reference services instructor. One of the assignments that I ask students to do is to ask a reference librarian a real reference question and reflect on the experience. Many students report back that they were worried that their questions were silly or that they were needlessly disturbing the librarian. Keep in mind that these are graduate students in library and information science who have, at minimum, a basic understanding of library services. So if they feel anxiety approaching the reference desk, imagine how a non–library professional must feel. Now add an additional layer of asking a personal health-related question—a question that is perhaps enveloped in stigma and shame. Is it any surprise that people aren't approaching our desks and openly asking about contraception, pregnancy, and sexuality?

Beyond search engines and complex questions, the lack of diversity in the library landscape no doubt plays a role in patron fears of approaching the reference desk. Let's look at the latest ALA membership survey: 86.7 percent of members identify as white, and only 4.7 percent reported their ethnicity as Hispanic or Latino. Additionally, a mere 4.4 percent of ALA members are Black or African American. Beyond this, 3.6 percent of ALA members are Asian and 1.2 percent are American Indian or Alaska Native. Native Hawaiian or Other Pacific Islander is a mere 0.2 percent.[3] Furthermore, only 2.91 percent of members reported that they have a disability. In terms of gender, the survey reported that 81 percent of members identify as female and 19 percent as male—it does not appear that the survey was made inclusive of other identity options, such as transgender male, transgender female, nonbinary, or gender variant/nonconforming.[4] Similarly, the US Census Bureau reports that librarians are 83 percent white.[5]

Given the homogeneity of the library profession, biases are bound to proliferate. These biases impact library services, programs, collections, and reference interactions. And they can certainly make for unwelcoming library environments. None of that bodes well for providing comprehensive sexual and reproductive health information.

Let's talk about biases. A bias is a "tendency, inclination, or prejudice toward or against something or someone" that is often based on stereotypes rather than "actual knowledge of an individual or circumstance."[6] Biases manifest as stereotypes held against groups of people and can be both conscious and unconscious. Effectively, we may claim to care deeply about diversity, equity, inclusion, accessibility, and belonging. Additionally, we may genuinely want to make our public library spaces more reflective of the communities that we serve and to be welcoming and open spaces. And yet our biases may prevent us from recognizing the gaps in our services, staffing, collections, and resources, including SRH information.

Therefore, providing adequate sexual and reproductive health information and services isn't just about buying more books or hosting more programs. In order to build a library space and environment where people can receive comprehensive SRH information, we librarians must do inner identity work so that we can approach these important topics thoughtfully. Such identity work will help us create more inclusive services and environments.

CIRCLES OF MY MULTICULTURAL SELF

Dr. Nicole A. Cooke's textbook *Information Services to Diverse Populations: Developing Culturally Competent Library Professionals* provides an overview of research and best practices for diversity and social justice in librarianship. Dr. Cooke also discusses cultural competency, social responsibility, and inner identity work. One of the practices outlined in the text references "Circles of My Multicultural Self," an activity during which participants process their own identities in order to discuss stereotypes and examine biases. I have found this to be a worthwhile exercise. You may want to explore how you can use this tool in your own identity work. Learn more at EdChange.org (www.edchange.org/multicultural/activities/circlesofself.html).

Reference Services

When I have connected with public librarians about sexual and reproductive health at the library, a common refrain has been that patrons do not come to the reference desk for SRH information. This isn't too surprising. How comfortable would you be going up to a stranger and asking them a question about your health—much less your sexual health? However, it is a mistake to attribute a lack of questions to a lack of interest. Many people may not ask out of fear or an assumption that the library doesn't have this information.

Part III: Implementation

Before we discuss reference interactions, let's first talk about how we can let our community know that their SRH queries are welcome. First, we can create shelf talkers about related databases and online resources so that people feel encouraged to seek out more information. Another option is to create more visible signage about different health topics. This could include a Tough Topics sign with call numbers to subjects that people may feel embarrassed to ask about at the reference desk.

At the reference desk, librarians should adhere to the guidelines for reference services provided by the Reference and User Services Association (RUSA). These include visibility/approachability, showing interest in patrons' needs, active listening and clarifying questions, searching, and follow-up. RUSA also outlines how to provide a quality reference interview. Of note for SRH information inquiries are sections 3.1.9 and 3.1.10, which state that a library worker "maintains objectivity; does not interject value judgments about the subject matter or the nature of the question into the transaction" and "respects patron privacy; maintains confidentiality after the transaction."[7] By providing SRH information, you are by no means expected to be an expert on this topic. However, as with the myriad other topical questions that patrons ask public librarians daily, we are expected to direct people to information and resources.

Special care should be taken with SRH reference questions. These steps can include moving the interaction to a more private space within the library, offering information in a variety of formats depending on the patron's information needs and abilities, refraining from making assumptions and judgments about the question, and ensuring that the patron feels satisfied with the information that they received.[8]

Librarians should never interpret medical information, make direct or indirect diagnoses, recommend health care procedures or practices, or refer patrons to specific health care providers. Libraries should consider posting both digital and printed disclaimers that explain how reference interactions are not a substitute for working with a health care provider or professional. And with the changing legal landscape surrounding topics like contraception, abortion, and LGBTQIA+ health issues, librarians should also ensure that they are not providing legal guidance.[9] You may want to practice with colleagues about how you can answer questions in a way that provides patrons with information

Chapter Seven: Sexual and Reproductive Health at Your Library

without giving guidance. I also recommend looking at RUSA's *Health and Medical Reference Guidelines* for more suggestions.[10]

Libraries should also look into incorporating chat, text, and e-mail platforms for people with accessibility or privacy concerns. Self-checkout machines and contactless pickups can also offer a degree of confidentiality. Furthermore, consider reminding patrons that public libraries do not keep records of materials checked out nor will libraries disclose this information to others.

HEALTH LITERACY

The US Department of Health and Human Services (HHS) defines personal health literacy as "the degree to which individuals have the ability to find, understand, and use information and services to inform health-related decisions and actions for themselves and others."[*] Health literacy includes one's ability to read and comprehend essential health-related materials, like prescription bottles and appointment slips. It also includes one's ability to take responsibility for their health and their family's health. HHS further defines organizational health literacy as "the degree to which organizations equitably enable individuals to find, understand, and use information and services to inform health-related decisions and actions for themselves and others."[†] Essentially, organizations, like libraries, can help advance health literacy. This guide is helping you do just that.

A 2022 report from the Milken Institute cited research which found that 88 percent of US adults have limited health literacy and 77 million Americans struggle with accessing health care services. These struggles are especially true for low-income individuals, those with disabilities, older adults, English language learners, and those with varying cultural beliefs.[‡]

Public librarians can work with patrons to find out the format of resources that work best for their information needs. Additionally, this is an opportunity to develop community partnerships and collaborations with health organizations. An article about how librarians can be key partners in health information includes peer training and

91

train-the-trainer models. In these cases, public librarians teach members of the community how to search for health information, like how to search the catalog or a database, how to find an article, and how to put a book on hold. In turn, those people can bring this new education to their networks.§

You can also learn more about health literacy from the American Medical Association Foundation's video on the topic (https://youtu.be/cGtTZ_vxjyA).

*"What Is Health Literacy?," Health Literacy, Centers for Disease Control and Prevention (CDC), last reviewed February 2, 2022, www.cdc.gov/healthliteracy/learn/index.html#:~:text=Personal%20health%20literacy%20is%20the,actions%20for%20themselves%20and%20others.

†"What Is Health Literacy?," CDC.

‡Claude Lopez, Bumyang Kim, and Katherine Sacks, *Health Literacy in the United States: Enhancing Assessments and Reducing Disparities* (Santa Monica, CA: Milken Institute, 2022), https://milkeninstitute.org/sites/default/files/2022-05/Health_Literacy_United_States_Final_Report.pdf.

§Wanda Whitney, Alla Keselman, and Betsy Humphreys, "Libraries and Librarians: Key Partners for Progress in Health Literacy Research and Practice," *Studies in Health Technology and Informatics* 240 (2017): 415–432.

Content Creation

Perhaps one of the most useful skills that you can take on for your library community is to get into the habit of curating content for your patrons. In most of the university classes that I teach, I almost always have an assignment that hinges on content creation or curation. This can be creating a resource guide, LibGuide, annotated bibliography, or tutorial or designing the outline for a workshop. But in doing this type of work, students are encouraged to consider how they aren't just introducing people to information; they are also instructors and facilitators of information. Additionally, the feedback that I often receive from students is that such activities help them better understand the resources that are available at the library and how they can communicate that information to patrons.

Resource guides and LibGuides are two popular creation methods. A resource guide is a collection of resources on a specific topic. These resource guides can direct patrons to databases, books, and relevant library programs/events. A resource guide can also include some information about how people can search the catalog or databases using specific keywords, filters, and subject headings. Free design tools like Canva can help librarians create attractive resource guides that can be printed and shared at the reference desk and linked on the website.

LibGuides are content management systems that librarians use to curate content and information on specific topics. These use widgets and other electronic tools to make them accessible and shareable on library websites. They are most common in university libraries. Whether you create a resource guide or utilize LibGuides, I recommend linking the resource in a place that is highly visible. For example, it may be helpful to have a link to different guides at the top of a database page.

SRH RESOURCE GUIDE IDEAS

The following list of resource guide topics are for you to contemplate when creating content for your library. Consider how you can weave together databases, fiction, nonfiction, magazines, media, and library events, programs, and workshops.

- consent and safety
- menstrual health
- miscarriages
- pregnancy options
- safe sex
- sexuality

For an idea of what general resource guides and LibGuides look like, see the examples available on ALA's website (www.ala.org/tools/topics/guides).

Tutorials

Where the resource guide provides a general overview about what information is available, the tutorial dives deeper into specific library resources. For example, a tutorial can be created to instruct people about how to search for sensitive topics in the library catalog or in the library databases. Another tutorial could include information about how people can access subject headings in databases or how they can assess credibility of a resource. You can also create tutorials in tandem with the resource guides; you can include a QR code that leads to the accompanying tutorial on the resource guide and place it in the stacks.

When creating tutorials, I recommend that you follow these basic practices:

- Focus on a very specific topic. Do not do a broad topic; keep it specific.
- Limit the tutorial to three to five minutes long. As yours will be a niche topic, keeping it limited shouldn't be too difficult. If you do have additional information that you'd like to include, create another quick video as a part 2.
- Put all the tutorials on a YouTube playlist for this specific topic or theme. This makes the content bingeable, and patrons will be able to navigate to the video that is most relevant to them.
- Embed the tutorial on your library website or include a link in a visible location, like on the databases page.
- Be sure to promote any accompanying resource guide to your video description on YouTube. You can include direct links to those resources.
- Use closed captions or an accompanying transcript so that the video is accessible to people with hearing impairments. You can enable automatic captions on YouTube or use Happy Scribe (www.happyscribe.com) for low-cost options for transcripts and subtitles.

These tutorials are important because they provide guidance to people who may otherwise be too afraid to go to the reference desk and ask for information.

Chapter Seven: Sexual and Reproductive Health at Your Library

CHOOSING YOUR SRH TUTORIAL TOPIC

Finding your niche topic for a tutorial can seem overwhelming, but ideas abound everywhere! I recommend that you start an idea file where you can jot down ideas when inspiration strikes you. For example, a patron may ask you a question that you realize would make a great tutorial. You can add that to the idea file and create tutorials that expand upon these questions and answers. Consider sharing the idea file with your colleagues so that you can work together to create new services, programs, and resources.

These questions may also help you figure out the theme for your next SRH tutorial:

- What do you wish that you had known about this topic?
- What are the common questions that you get asked on this topic or related ones?
- Which areas of the SRH collection circulate the most or the least? How can you incorporate those areas into a tutorial topic?
- What gaps do you see in the community or school curriculum and how can a tutorial close those gaps?
- Who is your target audience? What would they like to know?

Collection Development

In my own experience and in the conversations that I've had with public librarians, books on sexual and reproductive health information tend to be outdated and/or insufficient. The reason being is that these books are often an afterthought. And I get it—public librarians have a lot to handle, and it may be more efficient to purchase only popular books that are on the best-seller book lists and in book review journals. Plus, books on topics like STIs and sterilization aren't exactly beach reads or ones that you'll promote in a book talk. But that doesn't mean we should neglect adding them to our collections. Instead, we must consciously seek out these topics and add them to our collections. This book provides you with a variety of resources that you can use to get started.

Part III: Implementation

Depending on the policies at your library, parameters for weeding books are usually based on circulation numbers within a certain time frame. For example, your library may weed books that haven't circulated in three years or have circulated only once in two years, and so forth. When it comes to weeding books on SRH topics, I encourage you to take a different approach. After all, some people may not feel comfortable checking out such books from the library; perhaps they fear the judgment of library staff or that of their family members. For instance, someone who is in a relationship with an unsupportive or even abusive partner may not feel safe checking out certain material on a library card or bringing it home. This means that many people may come to the library to review the information that they need and then place the resources back on the shelves. Earlier in this book, I gave an example of someone doing just that. Please keep this in mind for these and other sensitive topics. Just because these resources aren't circulating outside of the library doesn't mean that they aren't being used in some capacity.

So how should a public librarian weed or update an SRH collection? I encourage you to see books on SRH information as a staple of your collection. In my opinion, this means that you should never be without them. They should be weeded and updated according to accuracy, currency, and relevancy. For instance, books about abortion prior to the US Supreme Court's reversal of *Roe v. Wade* in 2022 may now be outdated. You should scan the books for the type of language and content to make sure that they are current, inclusive, and up-to-date. I encourage you to set up a Google News Alert for SRH-related topics so that you can stay current on legislation.

I have worked in different public libraries with varying budgets, so I can appreciate the need to find a purchasing balance between popular material and core resources. I believe that the quality of books is more important than the quantity of books. So if you are able to purchase only a handful of books on these topics, that's a great way to get started! You may also find that this is an ideal opportunity to discuss interlibrary loan options, apply for a grant, or partner with a local community group or organization to make a more robust collection. Furthermore, you can promote any digital resources that can help people research these topics. Consider printing out quick reference guides on a variety of topics with instructions for how patrons can access more on these topics on their own.

Lastly, it is crucial to have strong collection development, library materials, challenged materials, and code of conduct policies. As most public librarians are aware, book challenges are at an all-time high. ALA's Office for Intellectual Freedom tracked 729 challenges to library, school, and university materials in 2021. This resulted in nearly 1,600 book challenges or removals—many of the targeted books were by or about Black or LGBTQIA+ people.[11] Staff training on how to best respond to patrons who are upset about library materials can help librarians feel supported and unified.

Above all, a collection that contains SRH information demonstrates to your community that you care about their access to these important topics. Learn more about policies and challenge support on ALA's website (www.ala.org/united/trustees/policies and www.ala.org/tools/challengesupport).

SRH COLLECTION DEVELOPMENT CHECKLIST

1. Review the books that you currently have on these topics: sexuality, sex education, sexually transmitted infections, pregnancy, abortion, miscarriage, menstrual health, contraception, and sterilization.
2. Determine when these books were published or acquired by your library. Using the explanations on these topics in this book as a guide, scan to see if these books are inclusive, accurate, and current.
3. If you need to update your collection, refer to the list of recommended resources in the appendix for suggestions as a way to get started. Additionally, look at legislation in your state regarding such topics as sexual education, abortion, and LGBTQIA+ concerns. Based on your findings, you can determine which specific gaps you can fill.
4. Review the subject headings and placement of these books in your collection. For example, LGBTQIA+ issues have historically been shelved along with topics related to pathologization and

criminalization. Additionally, books with religious viewpoints on sexual and reproductive health should be placed among other religious material.
5. Find ways that you can activate digital resources alongside the physical collection. This may include in-the-stacks signage promoting certain databases. Consider adding QR codes to this signage that link to tutorials and/or guides.
6. If you are including links to external health resources on your library's website, make sure to verify that these sources are credible. MedlinePlus provides a printable checklist (https://medlineplus.gov/webeval/webevalchecklist.html) with questions related to provider, funding, quality, and privacy. You can use this checklist when curating resources for your website, as well as in educating patrons about assessing health information.
7. If your budget allows, consider having two sets of SRH books: one that is available for circulation and one that is for in-library use only. This will allow information to be available even if other material is checked out.

Programs and Community Collaborations

Librarians are information professionals, not health care experts. So although we can direct people to resources and instruct them on how to search for information, we do not dive into the specifics on health topics. This is where we can partner with local organizations and associations to provide educational workshops and programs on such topics.

When seeking an organization to partner with, it is important to choose one that provides credible, evidence-based information. Possibilities include health departments; local universities, including nursing colleges and medical schools; hospitals; health care community groups; health associations and coalitions; and YMCAs. Topics may include comprehensive sex education, violence prevention, sexuality, pregnancy options, menstrual health, adoption, and pregnancy prevention. An important note about partnering with hospitals: although Catholic hospitals make up a significant percentage of hospitals throughout the

United States, including in rural and urban areas, they rarely provide information about or services related to sterilization, abortion, contraception, or LGBTQIA+ issues. Do keep this in mind when considering which hospitals you can collaborate with for educational programs.

You can also consider developing a partnership with local groups. For example, the Waukegan (IL) Public Library provides a monthly Health Awareness Series on hypertension, obesity, diabetes, and chronic diseases. These sessions are led by community health workers.[12] Additionally, at my own library, we hosted regular drop-in sessions with the local health department for dementia caregivers. Similar models could be created on SRH topics.

Furthermore, explore how your library can work with organizations on offering health care through the library. For instance, the COVID-19 pandemic ushered in a whole new era for telehealth appointments. These virtual meetings allow an individual to meet with their health care provider without going to an in-person visit. Depending on the service, telehealth appointments can be more affordable and more convenient. However, some people lack the technology and internet access to attend a telehealth visit in their homes. Libraries can provide space to make that happen.

The New York StateWide Senior Action Council (StateWide) and Oswego County Opportunities (OCO) did just that. In a coordinated effort, they teamed up to provide internet access and space for telehealth appointments as part of StateWide's larger Community Telehealth Access Project (CTAP). Maria Alvarez, StateWide's executive director, explained that this was a response to "the lack of equitable internet infrastructure across Central New York, which has left rural residents out of the telehealth boom, despite needing it the most due to transportation barriers and fewer local healthcare specialists in their communities."[13] Seven public libraries in Oswego County joined the initiative and, depending on their resources, were able to provide a private room, Wi-Fi, or devices.[14]

The Programming Librarian website has a list of ideas under "Health and Wellness" (https://programminglibrarian.org/tags/health-and-wellness). I recommend reviewing these program ideas and considering how you can make them relevant to SRH information. It is also helpful to have in place a firm programming policy about the types of programs that you provide and with whom you develop partnerships.

Part III: Implementation

SRH PROGRAM AND PARTNERSHIP IDEAS

SRH programs should be integrated into other health programs and workshops. This helps to destigmatize SRH events. For example, at my library, the following programs were held alongside those on such topics as osteoporosis, addiction, and dementia and a blood drive. And although they were new to the library and community, they were well received by those who attended.

- **Understanding Gynecological Cancer:** Otherwise known as the silent killer, ovarian cancer causes more deaths than any other cancer of the reproductive system. A licensed nurse will talk to you about warning signs, treatment options, and prevention for this and other gynecological cancers.
- **Sex Talk as Real Talk:** The earlier a parent begins an age-appropriate conversation with their children, the easier it is to talk with them about more difficult issues as their children approach adolescence. Learn how to clearly convey your expectations and values about sex and health in a calm and caring way.

Other ideas include integrating topics into book discussions, film screenings, and other educational series. When brainstorming ideas to add to your programming agenda, consider national and international observances, many of which can be found on the CDC's website (https://npin.cdc.gov/pages/annual-observances).

January
- Cervical Health Awareness Month

February
- International Prenatal Infection Prevention Month

March
- National Endometriosis Awareness Month
- Women's History Month
- National LGBT Health Awareness Week
- Transgender Day of Visibility

April
- STD Awareness Month
- Sexual Assault Awareness Prevention Month
- National Infertility Awareness Week
- Black Maternal Health Week
- Lesbian Visibility Day

May
- Preeclampsia Awareness Month
- National Women's Health Week
- National Women's Check-Up Day
- Menstrual Hygiene Day
- International Day Against Homophobia and Transphobia

June
- LGBTQIA+ Pride Month
- Men's Health Month
- National HIV Testing Day

July
- International Nonbinary People's Day

August
- National Breastfeeding Month
- World Breastfeeding Week

September
- Gynecologic Awareness Month
- Ovarian Cancer Awareness Month
- National Sexual Health Awareness Month
- Polycystic Ovary Syndrome Month
- World Sexual Health Day
- International Safe Abortion Day
- Celebrate Bisexuality Day

Part III: Implementation

October
- National Breast Cancer Awareness Month
- Metastatic Breast Cancer Awareness Day
- National Mammography Day
- National Domestic Violence Awareness Month
- International Day of the Girl
- LGBTQIA+ History Month
- Asexuality Awareness Week
- Intersex Awareness Day

November
- National Family Caregivers Day
- National Family Health History Day

December
- World AIDS Day

    When considering which organizations your library can partner with or what topics you can present on, you may find it helpful to conduct a community needs assessment. A community needs assessment can help you better understand what the people who live in your area actually need and want from the library. An assessment can inform you about languages that people speak, technology access, barriers to information and library access, and socioeconomic levels, as well as nonprofits, agencies, and associations in your area. You can get this information from both primary and secondary sources. For instance, you may look at census records or business reports. You may also get feedback through surveys, focus groups, or one-on-one conversations.

    Please note that when you are soliciting information from your community, you should explain how you plan to integrate feedback into library services. This work may seem complex, but it is important to building trust in your community and creating patron-centered services. The Community Tool Box from the University of Kansas (https://ctb.ku.edu/en) provides a plethora of resources, toolkits, and guides for developing community collaborations and conducting a needs assessment.

MENSTRUAL JUSTICE AT THE LIBRARY

EMILY ZERRENNER, a research and instruction librarian at Salisbury University, has been involved in menstrual justice throughout her academic career. In this interview, she discusses how libraries can address period poverty.

Q: How do you define menstrual justice?
Defining menstrual justice might be easier to first define what menstrual *injustice* is. Margaret E. Johnson defines it well in her paper "Menstrual Justice": "menstrual injustice is the oppression of menstruators, women, girls, transgender men and boys, and nonbinary persons simply because they menstruate" [https://scholarworks.law.ubalt.edu/all_fac/1089/]. Throughout history, there has been a heavy stigma on those who menstruate; one easy way to identify this is the many slang terms there are to refer to a menstrual cycle. Beyond the cultural ramifications, there is also a financial element. According to Anita Diamant in her book *Period. End of Sentence.*, period management can cost a person $17,000 over a lifetime; this includes things like pads, tampons, pain management, new underwear, et cetera. In the USA, there are some specific financial hardships as well. In many states, there is still a "tampon tax"—which refers to a sales or luxury tax on products like pads and tampons, adding cost to an already expensive necessity. By 2022, twenty-three states had specifically exempted period products from taxes [https://allianceforperiodsupplies.org/tampon-tax/]. Additionally, menstrual products aren't covered by WIC [Women, Infants, and Children] or SNAP [Supplemental Nutrition Assistance Program]. Only in 2020 were menstrual products allowed to be purchased with insurance accounts like HSAs [health savings accounts] and FSAs [flexible savings accounts]. To me, menstrual justice would mean we can talk freely about periods and the experience of menstruators, misinformation about how a menstrual cycle works would be corrected, and products related to menstrual management would be easy to obtain.

Q: Why should libraries care about menstrual justice?
Approximately half of the population menstruates, so given that, MANY of our patrons are dealing with this bodily function on a regular basis. Libraries are one of the last places where one can simply exist without paying, and they are generally trusted places for information. They are also historically a community hub—whether that community is a town, a college campus, or another gathering of people. With all of this combined, libraries are in a prime position to practice and promote menstrual justice.

Q: What steps can libraries take toward menstrual justice?
One step for libraries is to do what they do best: gather and promote resources on the subject. Some book suggestions are *Periods Gone Public: Taking a Stand for Menstrual Equity* by Jennifer Weiss-Wolf, *Period Power* by Nadya Okamoto, *The Managed Body* by Chris Bobel, *Period. End of Sentence.* by Anita Diamant, and the academic journal *Women's Reproductive Health* by the Society for Menstrual Health Research. Libraries can reach out to either their local organizations that do this kind of work to put on events or talks, or they can reach out to bigger national organizations about their booking policies too. Another is to absorb menstrual products into the already existing hygiene budget; libraries are already expected to provide things like toilet paper and hand soap in bathrooms, so what is the difference when it comes to menstrual products? The company Go Aunt Flow works with many types of organizations to install free menstrual product dispensers and disposal units for bathrooms; they may be a good tap for libraries. Ultimately, though, the first and most important step is to talk about it. Periods have a history of stigma; even the common product name, feminine hygiene, implies that one must keep their period clean and hidden (not to mention leaving out the many people who menstruate who don't identify as a woman).

Chapter Seven: Sexual and Reproductive Health at Your Library

Q: How can one organize/facilitate a menstrual product drive?
Organizing a menstrual product drive, first and foremost, needs planning. Why are you gathering products? Who are they for? Do you want only single-use products or will you accept things like menstrual cups? What kind of marketing and promotion will you create? Where are the prime locations to place a donation box in your organization? Are there local businesses or other organizations that can be a partner and also host a donation box? Are you going to have an online element, like an Amazon list of products needed, so that your nonlocal network might be able to participate too? Where are those products going to be shipped to? The drive I was a part of in undergrad was gathering products for local middle schools, so another element to our drive was to gather small bags and/or purses to place the products in. We held an event where any students were welcome to come assemble those bags, and I put on a presentation about more sustainable period product options, like menstrual cups and cloth pads. It was LIB 200 approved, which meant students could come and write about it for a class assignment. Work out these sorts of details, have a clear beginning and end date, and then you can get started with the product drive.

Q: Why should we be talking about periods now?
It's even more important now to talk about periods and how they work given the reversal of *Roe v. Wade*. There is so much misinformation out there; menstruators and nonmenstruators alike both need to know how to track periods to adequately prevent pregnancy. For example, with a six-week abortion ban, for an average menstruator that means only two weeks after a missed period. Even though there are many apps that help you track your period, the data privacy issues related to them make me hesitant in suggesting them. A paper calendar method is probably best at this time.   ● ● ● ● ●

> ## CONTINUING EDUCATION
>
> The following are some organizations where you can access resources so that you can continue to educate yourself on health information and topics:
>
> - **The Network of the National Library of Medicine** (NNLM; https://nnlm.gov) has a wealth of guides, resources, trainings, funding, and initiatives. NNLM's handout *Helping Public Libraries Meet Community Health Needs* (https://nnlm.gov/sites/default/files/2021-11/PublicLibrariesHandout_2021Sept.pdf) is especially useful.
> - **The Centers for Disease Control and Prevention** offers a variety of resources for library professionals and their partners. This includes a collaboration toolkit and training resources (www.cdc.gov/healthliteracy/education-support/libraries.html).
> - **The Public Library Association** has a website on health literacy, programming, and consumer health information (www.ala.org/pla/initiatives/healthliteracy). This includes an on-demand webinar about community health in public libraries, as well as access to the PLA Health Interest Group.

Final Thoughts

I hope that this chapter leaves you with a better understanding as to why people may not feel comfortable asking for SRH-related information. Additionally, I hope you have a newfound appreciation for the importance of identity work. It is through identity work that we can better understand our biases and how these may impact the services and information that we do or do not provide. When we recognize our biases, we can confront them and work toward dismantling systems that are unjust, including those with a lack of sexual and reproductive health information.

Chapter Seven: Sexual and Reproductive Health at Your Library

Let's Review

- The lack of SRH information in libraries may partly be because patrons do not ask for this information. However, this doesn't mean that they aren't looking for it. Patrons may be afraid to ask librarians for personal information, especially if the library space is unwelcoming. This creates a vicious cycle in which librarians assume that SRH information is not a priority and patrons are met with inadequate SRH resources and services.
- When providing reference services for health information, we should ensure patron privacy and confidentiality. This may include adding virtual reference options.
- Content creation efforts like resource guides and tutorials can introduce people to and empower them to use the resources that the library has available.
- Collections for SRH information should be regularly reviewed for accuracy, currency, and inclusivity. When weeding materials, be mindful that many people may use the resources only in the library, and circulation statistics may therefore be lower than actual use.
- Community collaborations can provide an opportunity for public libraries to facilitate access to health information on a local level. These may include working with local health care organizations that can provide traditional presentations and informational partnerships.
- Libraries can help advance menstrual justice by providing free period resources in the bathroom, participating in a menstrual product drive, and hosting discussions about menstrual health.

Reflection Questions

1. List two to three topics that you can focus on to create tutorials and resource guides. How can these complement your physical and digital collections?
2. Are there any local opportunities to participate in a menstrual product drive or provide menstrual products? Discuss with your colleagues. You can get more ideas at MenstrualHygieneDay.org.
3. Which local organizations can you partner with for programs, workshops, or other collaborations related to SRH? Brainstorm a list with colleagues and then develop a plan for reaching out to these groups to discuss opportunities.

Part III: Implementation

NOTES

1. Constance A. Mellon, "Library Anxiety: A Grounded Theory and Its Development," *College and Research Libraries* 47, no. 2 (1986): 160–65, https://doi.org/10.5860/crl_47_02_160.
2. John Walsh, *Information Literacy Instruction: Selecting an Effective Model*, Chandos Information Professional Series (Oxford, UK: Chandos Publishing, 2011).
3. "Librarian Ethnicity," American Library Association, www.ala.org/tools/librarian-ethnicity.
4. ALA Office for Research and Statistics, *2017 ALA Demographic Study* (Chicago: ALA, 2017).
5. "Library Professionals: Facts, Figures, and Union Membership," 2021 Fact Sheet, Department for Professional Employees, June 10, 2021, www.dpeaflcio.org/factsheets/library-professionals-facts-and-figures.
6. "Bias," Psychology Today, www.psychologytoday.com/us/basics/bias.
7. RUSA (Reference and User Services Association), "Guidelines for Behavioral Performance of Reference and Information Service Providers," American Library Association, www.ala.org/rusa/resources/guidelines/guidelinesbehavioral.
8. RUSA, "Guidelines for Behavioral Performance."
9. Maura Sostack and Rebecca Davis, "Health and Medicine Sources," In *Reference and Information Services: An Introduction*, 6th ed, eds. Melissa A. Wong and Laura Saunders (Santa Barbara, CA: Libraries Unlimited, 2020), 631–59.
10. RUSA (Reference and User Services Association), "Health and Medical Reference Guidelines," American Library Association, www.ala.org/rusa/resources/guidelines/guidelinesmedical.
11. ALA News, "National Library Week Kicks Off with State of America's Libraries Report, Annual Top 10 Most Challenged Books List, and a New Campaign to Fight Book Bans," American Library Association, April 4, 2022, www.ala.org/news/press-releases/2022/04/national-library-week-kicks-state-america-s-libraries-report-annual-top-10.
12. "Health Awareness," Waukegan Public Library, www.waukeganpl.org/learning-2/health-awareness/.
13. "Telehealth Access Portal Opens at OCO Fulton Office," Oswego County Opportunities (OCO), August 5, 2021, www.oco.org/oco-news/telehealth-access-portal-opens-at-oco-fulton-office/.
14. "Telehealth Access Portal," OCO.

CHAPTER EIGHT

Moving Forward

WE'VE COME QUITE a long way! Throughout the previous seven chapters, we really dove into how you can advocate for sexual and reproductive health information at your public library. Additionally, we explored how you can make connections to your library through reference, content creation, collection development, and community collaborations. With all of this information, you may feel overwhelmed. Therefore, this is the perfect opportunity to coalesce these concepts.

Putting It All Together

We started this book by discussing the core foundation of sexual and reproductive health. We talked about different definitions and meanings, including specific SRH concepts that we would focus on for the purposes of this book. We also introduced the reproductive justice framework. RJ is a holistic lens into how people can maintain bodily autonomy, have children, not have children, and raise children in safe communities. Lastly, we discussed the historical background of sexual and reproductive health in the United States, including barriers and inequalities that make it more important for public libraries to provide information access to these crucial topics.

We made this connection in the second chapter where we learned how SRH information is aligned with library values, guidelines, and practices. We further explored how access to SRH information is a human right and a component of the United Nations' Sustainable

Development Goals. We also considered how librarianship upholds intellectual freedom and information access. Additionally, we discussed sexuality and concepts related to sexual orientation and gender, as well as the intersection of sexuality and health.

Moving along, we dove into specific SRH concepts. This included information about contraception, sterilization, and sexually transmitted infections. The discussion also incorporated reproductive health concepts, like menstruation, menopause, pregnancy options, and cancers. That led us to a conversation about how we can ensure that our sexual and reproductive health services and information are also inclusive of LGBTQIA+ patrons. By thinking beyond heteronormative concepts, we can work toward a library environment where all people feel comfortable learning about their health.

Finally, we connected these themes together in a way that allows us to integrate these information services into our existing library work. However, in order to provide such services, we must understand the power dynamics that exist between the librarian and the patron. Examining our own biases and understanding our positionality in regard to the community can help us do that. It is also imperative that we understand patron anxiety and how this may prevent people from approaching the reference desk and asking questions about sexual and reproductive health.

Creating a welcoming environment with a variety of reference platforms can help facilitate those inquiries. This endeavor may include considering how we provide collection development and reference services, developing community partnerships and collaborations for patron education, and creating spaces and resources for our libraries that ensure people can access the information that they need in a way that feels most comfortable for them. We discussed the importance of strong library policies and how community partnerships may take on a variety of formats.

As you provide SRH information, it is important to continue your education. While you are not expected to be a health expert, it can be beneficial to your community if you understand the legal landscape in your state and can add evidence-based resources and partnerships to your roster. We discussed some key websites and organizations that you can utilize for learning. This book also provides recommended resources in the appendix that you can use to begin to make this happen at your library.

Next Steps

At this point you may feel energized, nervous, uncertain, or any combination of these emotions about how to move forward. Please know that these feelings are normal for taking on any new library service or initiative. If you are unsure of how to get started or need a healthy dose of inspiration, here are some suggestions:

- Make a short list of organizations and community groups with which you would like to develop SRH partnerships. Consider how you can connect with them for informational interviews and to discuss future opportunities.
- Subscribe to news alerts so that you can stay informed about these topics on local, state, and national levels. Being informed can help you better determine what resources your library can provide.
- Create an idea file. If you're anything like me, ideas come at the oddest moments. This file can help you quickly jot down topics for the collection, tutorials, or programs for future use. Refer to this when you need inspiration.
- Watch a webinar or read an article from any of the resources in this book. Get comfortable talking about what you learned with others, like your family or friends. This will help destigmatize these often-taboo topics.
- Meet with other librarians in your community or network. Brainstorm ideas about how you can integrate these concepts into your library work and how you can provide support to one another when engaged in larger initiatives.

Being Bold

You have all the tools, resources, and information that you need to get started in providing services for sexual and reproductive health information at your library. But don't worry about doing it all at once! Take the steps that feel most comfortable and manageable. You can then move forward in the ways that make sense for you and your library.

As you get going, you will learn more about how you can show up for your library community in a way that makes sense. After all, every library and library community is different, so these services are not going to be identical in each and every public library that employs them. I encourage you to have regular conversations with your team about how SRH services and information can be incorporated at your library now and in the future. However this model looks for your library and patrons, know that your actions are important and necessary. Essentially, you are making bold moves for the people whom you serve. You should commend yourself for stepping up to the plate to make this happen.

Concluding Thoughts

I hope that this book has left you feeling encouraged, energized, and supported. Please consider this book as not only a guide but also a partner in your practice. The SRH information and related checklists, ideas, and resources will be here for you when you need them. Ideally, this book will serve as a portal to more in-depth readings and discussions on these specific topics. Never has there been a more necessary time to provide sexual and reproductive health information to our communities. And you are more than ready to move forward.

APPENDIX

Recommended Resources

These resources can help you with both your own continued education and curation for your library collection. Please note that this is not an exhaustive list. There are plenty more resources out there, but the ones listed here, organized by topic, should be sufficient to introduce you to further information on these topics.

Library-Related Resources, Organizations, and Articles

American Library Association Gay, Lesbian, Bisexual, and Transgender Round Table. *Open to All: Serving the GLBT Community in Your Library* (toolkit). Chicago: ALA GLBTRT, n.d. www.ala.org/rt/sites/ala.org.rt/files/content/professionaltools/160309-glbtrt-open-to-all-toolkit-online.pdf.

Betts-Green, Dawn. "We Could Do Better": Librarian Engagement in LGBTQ Collection Development in Small and Rural Public Libraries in the Southern U.S." *Public Library Quarterly* 39, no. 6 (2020): 510–36. https://doi.org/10.1080/01616846.2020.1737493.

Cooke, Nicole A. *Information Services to Diverse Populations: Developing Culturally Competent Library Professionals.* Santa Barbara, CA: Libraries Unlimited, 2016.

Defending Intellectual Freedom: LGBTQ+ Materials in School Libraries (National School Library Standards). Chicago: American Association of School Librarians, n.d. https://standards.aasl.org/project/lgbtq/.

Dorr, Christina H., Liz Deskins, and Jamie Campbell Naidoo. *LGBTQAI+ Books for Children and Teens: Providing a Window for All.* Chicago: ALA Editions, 2018.

Appendix

"Equity, Diversity, and Inclusion" (web page). American Library Association. www.ala.org/advocacy/diversity.

Ettarh, Fobazzi. "Vocational Awe and Librarianship: The Lies We Tell Ourselves." *In the Library with the Lead Pipe,* January 10, 2018. www.inthelibrarywiththeleadpipe.org/2018/vocational-awe/.

Hathcock, April. "White Librarianship in Blackface: Diversity Initiatives in LIS." *In the Library with the Lead Pipe,* October 7, 2015.

Hughes, Kathleen. "Knowledge Is Power: Serving Gender Diverse Youth in the Library." Public Libraries Online, May 11, 2016.

Mellon, Constance A. "Library Anxiety: A Grounded Theory and Its Development." *College and Research Libraries* 47, no. 2 (1986): 160–65. https://doi.org/10.5860/crl_47_02_160.

"Multicultural Education Pavilion—Diversity, Equity, and Social Justice Education Resources" (web page). EdChange. www.edchange.org/multicultural/index.html.

Nordell, Jessica. *The End of Bias a Beginning: The Science and Practice of Overcoming Unconscious Bias.* New York: Metropolitan Books, 2021.

Zettervall, Sara K., and Mary C. Nienow. *Whole Person Librarianship: A Social Work Approach to Patron Services.* Santa Barbara, CA: Libraries Unlimited, 2019.

Reproductive and Sexual Health
Books

Baum, Neil, and Scott Miller. *How's It Hanging? Expert Answers to the Questions Men Don't Always Ask.* La Vergne, TN: Skyhorse, 2018.

Boston Women's Health Collective. *Our Bodies, Ourselves.* New York: Simon & Schuster, 2011.

Foster, Diana Greene. *The Turnaway Study: Ten Years, a Thousand Women, and the Consequences of Having—or Being Denied—an Abortion.* New York: Scribner, 2021.

Gunter, Jen. *The Menopause Manifesto: Own Your Health with Facts and Feminism.* Toronto: Random House Canada, 2021.

———. *The Vagina Bible: The Vulva and the Vagina—Separating the Myth from the Medicine.* New York: Citadel Press, 2019.

Hill, Maisie. *Perimenopause Power: Navigating Your Hormones on the Journey to Menopause.* London: Green Tree, 2021.

Marty, Robin. *New Handbook for a Post-Roe America: The Complete Guide to Abortion Legality, Access, and Practical Support.* New York: Seven Stories Press, 2021.

O'Toole, Elisabeth. *In on It: What Adoptive Parents Would Like You to Know about Adoption: A Guide for Relatives and Friends.* St. Paul, MN: Fig Press, 2011.

Parker, Lara. *Vagina Problems: Endometriosis, Painful Sex, and Other Taboo Topics.* New York: St. Martin's Griffin, 2020.

Roorda, Rhonda M. *In Their Voices: Black Americans on Transracial Adoption.* New York: Columbia University Press, 2015.

Spitz, Aaron. *The Penis Book: A Doctor's Complete Guide to the Penis—from Size to Function and Everything in Between.* Emmaus, PA: Rodale, 2018.

Walbert, David F., and J. Douglas Butler. *Whose Choice Is It? Abortion, Medicine, and the Law.* Chicago: American Bar Association, 2021.

Weiss-Wolf, Jennifer. *Periods Gone Public: Taking a Stand for Menstrual Equity.* New York: Arcade, 2017.

Wick, Myra J. *Mayo Clinic Guide to a Healthy Pregnancy.* 2nd ed. Rochester, MN: Mayo Clinic Press, 2018.

Your Pregnancy and Childbirth: Month to Month. 7th ed. Washington, DC: American College of Obstetricians and Gynecologists, 2021.

Online Resources

ASHA American Sexual Health Association. www.ashasexualhealth.org.
———. *Sex + Health* (podcast). https://soundcloud.com/asha_sexual_health.
CDC Centers for Disease Control and Prevention. "Reproductive Health." www.cdc.gov/reproductivehealth/index.html.
Guttmacher Institute. www.guttmacher.org.
Healthy People 2030 (microsite). Office of Disease Prevention and Health Promotion, US Department of Health and Human Services. https://health.gov/healthypeople.
Ibis Reproductive Health. www.ibisreproductivehealth.org.
Kaiser Family Foundation. "KFF—Health Policy Analysis, Polling, Journalism and Social Impact Media." www.kff.org.
NIRH National Institute for Reproductive Health. www.nirhealth.org.

Office on Women's Health (website). Office of the Assistant Secretary for Health, US Department of Health and Human Services. www.womenshealth.gov.
Pad Project, The. https://thepadproject.org.
PRH Physicians for Reproductive Health. https://prh.org.
Sex & U. Society of Obstetricians and Gynaecologists of Canada. www.sexandu.ca.
SexEd Library. www.sexedlibrary.org.
WHO World Health Organization. "Sexual and Reproductive Health and Research (SRH)." www.who.int/teams/sexual-and-reproductive-health-and-research-(srh)/overview.

Reproductive Justice

Books

Briggs, Laura. *Reproducing Empire: Race, Sex, Science, and U.S. Imperialism in Puerto Rico.* Berkeley: University of California Press, 2006.

Gurr, Barbara Anne. *Reproductive Justice: The Politics of Health Care for Native American Women.* New Brunswick, NJ: Rutgers University Press, 2015.

Luna, Zakiya. *Reproductive Rights as Human Rights: Women of Color and the Fight for Reproductive Justice.* New York: New York University Press, 2020.

Roberts, Dorothy E. *Killing the Black Body: Race, Reproduction, and the Meaning of Liberty.* New York: Vintage, 1999.

Ross, Loretta, Lynn Roberts, Erika Derkas, Whitney Peoples, Pamela Bridgewater Toure, and Dorothy Roberts. *Radical Reproductive Justice: Foundation, Theory, Practice, Critique.* New York: Feminist Press, 2017.

Ross, Loretta, and Rickie Solinger. *Reproductive Justice: An Introduction.* Berkeley: University of California Press, 2017.

Silliman, Jael, Marlene Gerber Fried, Loretta Ross, and Elena R. Gutiérrez. *Undivided Rights: Women of Color Organizing for Reproductive Justice.* Chicago: Haymarket Books, 2016.

Online Resources

In Our Own Voice—National Black Women's Reproductive Justice Agenda. https://blackrj.org.
Indigenous Women Rising. www.iwrising.org.

National Women's Law Center. "Reproductive Justice Archives." https://nwlc.org/issue/reproductive-justice/.

SisterSong Women of Color Reproductive Justice Collective. www.sistersong.net.

Sexuality and LGBTQIA+ Health
Books

Eckstrand, Kristen, and Jesse M. Ehrenfeld, eds. *Lesbian, Gay, Bisexual, and Transgender Healthcare: A Clinical Guide to Preventive, Primary, and Specialist Care.* Cham, Switzerland: Springer International, 2018.

Gainsburg, Jeannie. *The Savvy Ally: A Guide for Becoming a Skilled LGBTQ+ Advocate.* Lanham, MD: Rowman & Littlefield, 2020.

Langford, Jo. *The Pride Guide: A Guide to Sexual and Social Health for LGBTQ Youth.* Lanham, MD: Rowman & Littlefield, 2020.

Madrone, Kelly Huegel. *LGBTQ: The Survival Guide for Lesbian, Gay, Bisexual, Transgender, and Questioning Teens.* Minneapolis, MN: Free Spirit, 2019.

Pessin-Whedbee, Brook, and Naomi Bardoff. *Who Are You? The Kid's Guide to Gender Identity.* London: Jessica Kingsley, 2017.

Sharman, Zena. *The Remedy: Queer and Trans Voices on Health and Health Care.* Vancouver, BC: Arsenal Pulp Press, 2018.

Tando, Darlene. *The Conscious Parent's Guide to Gender Identity: A Mindful Approach to Embracing Your Child's Authentic Self.* Avon, MA: Adams Media, 2016.

Vincent, Ben. *Transgender Health: A Practitioner's Guide to Binary and Non-binary Trans Patient Care.* London: Jessica Kingsley, 2018.

Online Resources

"Know Your Rights: LGBTQ Rights." American Civil Liberties Union. www.aclu.org/know-your-rights/lgbtq-rights.

"LGBTQ Resource List." GLAAD. www.glaad.org/resourcelist.

"LGBT[Q] Youth Resources." Centers for Disease Control and Prevention. www.cdc.gov/lgbthealth/youth-resources.htm.

"PFLAG National Glossary of Terms." PFLAG. https://pflag.org/glossary.

Appendix

Organizations

Asexual Visibility & Education Network. www.asexuality.org.
GLAAD. www.glaad.org.
GLMA: Health Professionals Advancing LGBTQ Equality. www.glma.org.
Human Rights Campaign. www.hrc.org.
interACT: Advocates for Intersex Youth. https://interactadvocates.org.
MAP Movement Advancement Project. www.lgbtmap.org.
National Coalition for LGBTQ Health. https://healthlgbt.org.
National LGBTQIA+ Health Education Center. www.lgbtqiahealtheducation.org.
National LGBTQ Task Force. www.thetaskforce.org.
PFLAG. https://pflag.org.
Trevor Project, The. www.thetrevorproject.org.
World Professional Association for Transgender Health. www.wpath.org.

Magazines

Advocate. www.advocate.com.
Lavender Magazine. https://lavendermagazine.com.
Out. www.out.com.
Them. www.them.us.

Sexual Pleasure and Consent

Archambault, Julie. *Sex Up Your Life: The Mind-Blowing Path to True Intimacy, Healing, and Hope.* Vancouver, BC: CoCreative Press, 2020.
Liu, Vic, ed. *Bang! Masturbation for People of All Genders and Abilities.* Portland, OR: Microcosm, 2021.
Maltz, Wendy. *The Sexual Healing Journey: A Guide for Survivors of Sexual Abuse.* New York: William Morrow, 2012.
Mintz, Laurie B. *Becoming Cliterate: Why Orgasm Equality Matters—and How to Get It.* New York: HarperOne, 2018.
Moon, Allison. *Getting It: A Guide to Hot, Healthy Hookups and Shame-Free Sex.* Berkeley, CA: Ten Speed Press, 2021.
Nagoski, Emily. *Come as You Are: The Surprising New Science That Will Transform Your Sex Life.* New York: Simon and Schuster Paperbacks, 2022.

Roche, Juno. *Queer Sex: A Trans and Non-binary Guide to Intimacy, Pleasure and Relationships.* London: Jessica Kingsley, 2018.

Snyder, Stephen. *Love Worth Making: How to Have Ridiculously Great Sex in a Long-Lasting Relationship.* New York: St. Martin's Griffin, 2019.

Sexual and Reproductive Health Databases

Archives of Sexual Behavior. https://www.springer.com/journal/10508. From the International Academy of Sex Research, this database includes research, essays, case reports, and book reviews.

Centers for Disease Control and Prevention. "Databases for Public Health Research." www.cdc.gov/dhdsp/maps/gisx/resources/phr-databases.html. This web page provides links to open databases and online directories for continued education and research.

GenderWatch. ProQuest. https://about.proquest.com/en/products-services/genderwatch/. Access more than 219,000 full articles for research based on gender, women's studies, and LGBTQIA+ concepts.

Global Health. "The Global Health Database for the Public Health Digital Library." CABI.org. https://www.cabi.org/products-and-services/the-global-health-database-for-the-public-health-digital-library/. This database includes more than 4.3 million records related to public health research and practice, including international health.

International Journal of Transgender Health. www.tandfonline.com/journals/wijt21. In partnership with the World Professional Association for Transgender Health, this journal includes a variety of research articles related to sexual and reproductive health. Check your library's scholarly database for access.

LGBTQ+ Source. EBSCO. www.ebsco.com/products/research-databases/lgbtq-source. This full-text database includes scholarly and popular LGBTQIA+ publications, including magazines and newspapers.

PubMed. https://pubmed.ncbi.nlm.nih.gov. This database offers access to more than 33 million citations for journal articles, literature, and online books.

Scopus. www.scopus.com/home.uri. This abstract and citation database covers nearly 35,000 peer-reviewed journals on life, social, physical, and health sciences.

Index

A

AASL (American Association of School Librarians), 113
Abbott, Greg, 8
abortion
    Crisis Pregnancy Centers and, 61–62
    Native American women and, 6
    overview of, 59–61
    in reproductive health care, 66
    resources on, 114, 115
    Roe v. Wade, reversal of, 60, 105
    spontaneous abortions, 58
    SRH collection development checklist, 97
    SRH information, lack of access to, 16
    sterilization and, 35
    weeding of collection, 96
"Access to Library Resources and Services" (American Library Association), 13
Accord Alliance website, 51
ACLU (American Civil Liberties Union), 117
acquired immunodeficiency syndrome (AIDS), 38–39
adenomyosis, 51, 54
adoption
    information about, 59
    resources about, 115
Advocate magazine, 118
AIS (androgen insensitivity syndrome), 51
ALA
    See American Library Association
Alvarez, Barbara A., x–xi
Alvarez, Maria, 99
AMA Journal of Ethics, 39, 62
amenorrhea, 50

American Academy of Pediatrics, 79
American Association of School Librarians (AASL), 113
American Civil Liberties Union (ACLU), 117
American College of Obstetricians and Gynecologists
    on abortion reversal treatments, 60
    on sterilization, 35
    support of abortion, 61
    website of, 51
    Your Pregnancy and Childbirth: Month to Month, 115
American College of Physicians, 61
American Journal of Public Health, 79
American Library Association (ALA)
    on access to information, 13–14
    "Equity, Diversity, and Inclusion" web page, 114
    Freedom to Read Statement, 14
    for LibGuide examples, 93
    membership, demographics of, 88
    Office for Intellectual Freedom, 97
    policies/challenge support information, 97
    SRH information access and, 17
American Library Association Gay, Lesbian, Bisexual, and Transgender Round Table (ALA GLBTRT), 113
American Medical Association, 61
American Sexual Health Association, 39, 115
androgen insensitivity syndrome (AIS), 51
antiobscenity laws, 33–34
antisodomy laws, 75
anxiety, library, 87–89

Index

Archambault, Julie, 118
Archives of Sexual Behavior (database), 119
Article 19, UDHR, 15
articles, library-related, 113–114
asexual people
    definition of, 24
    diagnosis of, 72
    See also LGBTQIA+ community
Asexual Visibility & Education Network, 118

B

Baird, Eisenstadt v., 34
Bang! Masturbation for People of All Genders and Abilities (Liu), 118
Bardoff, Naomi, 117
barrier birth control, 34, 38
Baum, Neil, 114
Becoming Cliterate: Why Orgasm Equality Matters—and How to Get It (Mintz), 118
Bell, Buck v., 7
Betts-Green, Dawn, 113
bias
    in public library services, 87–89
    understanding, 106, 110
Biden, Joe, 74
birth control, 34
    See also contraception
birth control implants, 34
birth control pill
    for endometriosis treatment, 53–54
    menstruation and, 50
    testing of, 6
birthing options, 58
bisexual people
    definition of, 24
    health care system and, 74
Black Americans
    disparities in quality of health care for, 14–15
    lack of diversity in libraries, 88
    reproductive justice for, lack of, 5, 7–8, 9
BMC Women's Health, 51
Bobel, Chris, 104
bodily autonomy
    of Black women in U.S., 7–8
    as part of sexual and reproductive health, 4, 9
    reproductive justice, 6
    sterilization and, 6–7
book challenges, 97

books
    on menstrual justice, 104
    on reproductive and sexual health, 114–115
    on reproductive justice, 116
    on sexuality/LGBTQIA health, 117
Boston Women's Health Collective, 114
breast cancer, 62–63
breast health, 62–63
breastfeeding, 63–64
Briggs, Laura, 116
Buck v. Bell, 7
Burke, Tarana, 41
Butler, J. Douglas, 115

C

calendar, 100–102
California, 7
cancers
    breast cancer, 62–63
    gynecologic cancers, 65
    prostate cancer, 63
    reproductive health-related cancers, 66
    SRH program/partnership ideas, 100
    testicular/penile cancer, 64–65
Canva, 93
Carlson, Carolyn, 14
Catholic hospitals, 98
censorship, 97
Centers for Disease Control and Prevention (CDC)
    on abortions, 60
    on breastfeeding, 63
    "Databases for Public Health Research," 119
    on health literacy, 91–92
    on importance of SRH information, 17
    "LGBT[Q] Youth Resources," 117
    on LGBTQIA+ youth, 75
    on national/international observances, 100
    pap testing recommendation, 65
    on pregnancy-related deaths, 8
    on prostate cancer, 64
    on rape survivors, 41
    "Reproductive Health" resource, 115
    resources for continuing education, 106
    STI Treatment Guidelines Timeline, 36, 37
    on STIs in U.S., 38
    STOP SV: A Technical Package to Prevent Sexual Violence, 42

Index

cervical cancer, 65
cervical caps, 34
checklist, SRH collection development, 97
children
    adoption of, 59
    intersex individuals, 73
    LGBTQIA+, support of, 80
    LGBTQIA+ community, denial of care, 8
    reproductive justice and, 6, 36
    Sex Talk As Real Talk program, 100
    sexual and reproductive health rights and, 4
chlamydia, 38
"Circles of My Multicultural Self" activity, 89
circulation numbers, 96
cisgender, 21
Cleveland Clinic
    on birthing options, 58
    on preeclampsia, 56
    on uterine fibroids, 54
    website of, 52
closed captions, 94
clothing
    gender norms through time, 23
    sexual violence and, 42
    transition and, 76
collaboration
    community collaborations for SRH program, 107
    for SRH programs, 98–102
    See also partnerships
collection development
    SRH information access and, 14
    SRH information integration into library, 95–98
"The Color System," 43
Come as You Are: The Surprising New Science That Will Transform Your Sex Life (Nagoski), 118
communication, 39
community
    collaborations for SRH programs, 98–102, 107
    library as community center, 16
    library SRH services for, 112
community needs assessment, 102
Community Telehealth Access Project (CTAP), 99
Community Tool Box, 102
Comstock Act, 34
conception
    fertility/infertility, 56–57
    process of, 55
condoms
    for LGBTQIA+ people, 80
    most popular types of birth control, 34
    sex education in schools about, 40
    for STI prevention, 38
confidentiality, 90–91
Connecticut, Griswold v., 34
The Conscious Parent's Guide to Gender Identity: A Mindful Approach to Embracing Your Child's Authentic Self (Tando), 117
consent
    definition of, 39
    resources on, 118–119
    sexual violence and, 41
content creation, 92–93
continuing education
    resources for, 106
    on SRH information, 110
contraception
    history of, 32–34
    lack of access to, 16
    LGBTQIA+ people and, 74, 79–80
    for prevention of STIs, 38
    review of, 44
    sex education in schools about, 40
contraceptive sponges, 34
conversion therapy, 72–73
Cooke, Nicole A., 89, 113
court cases
    Buck v. Bell, 7
    Eisenstadt v. Baird, 34
    Griswold v. Connecticut, 34
    Lawrence v. Texas, 75
    Obergefell v. Hodges, 75
    Roe v. Wade, 60, 96
    United States v. One Package, 34
COVID-19 pandemic
    intimate partner violence during, 42
    library health care programs, 99
Crenshaw, Kimberlé, 25, 26
Crisis Pregnancy Centers, 61–62
CTAP (Community Telehealth Access Project), 99

D

databases, sexual and reproductive health, 119
"Databases for Public Health Research" (CDC), 119

Index

Defending Intellectual Freedom: LGBTQ+ Materials in School Libraries (National School Library Standards) (AASL), 113
Defense of Marriage Act (DOMA), 74–75
demisexual, 24
demystify, x
Derkas, Erika, 116
Deskins, Liz, 113
Diagnostic and Statistical Manual of Mental Disorders (DSM-1) (American Psychiatric Association), 71, 72
Diamant, Anita, 103, 104
diaphragm, 34
diversity, 88
"Don't Say Gay" legislation, 40
Dorr, Christina H., 113
dysmenorrhea (menstrual pain), 50–51

E

EBSCO, 119
Eckstrand, Kristen, 117
ectopic pregnancy, 55–56
EdChange.org, 89, 114
education
    continuing education, 106, 110
    LGBTQIA+ sexual and reproductive health topics, 71–81
    on reproductive health, 49–66
    on sexual health, 31–44
egg
    ectopic pregnancy, 55–56
    egg freezing/embryo creation, 78
    fertilization of, 55, 57
Egypt, 32–33
Ehrenfeld, Jesse M., 117
Eisenstadt v. Baird, 34
Embedded Business Librarianship for the Public Librarian (Alvarez), x
emergency contraception (EC), 34
The End of Bias a Beginning: The Science and Practice of Overcoming Unconscious Bias (Nordell), 114
endometriosis
    hysterectomy for, 54
    secondary dysmenorrhea from, 51
    symptoms of/treatment of, 53–54
"Equity, Diversity, and Inclusion" (web page), 114
Ettarh, Fobazzi, 114

F

Failey, Tara, 35–36
fallopian tubes, 35
FDA (Food and Drug Administration), 34
feedback, 102
fertility, 56
fibroids, 51
First Amendment, 14, 17
Food and Drug Administration (FDA), 34
Foster, Diana Greene, 114
four pillars of comprehensive public health approach to sexuality, 32, 33
freedom of speech, 62
Freedom to Read Statement (American Library Association), 14, 17
Fried, Marlene Gerber, 116

G

Gainsburg, Jeannie, 117
Gay & Lesbian Alliance Against Defamation (GLAAD), 117, 118
gay people
    definition of, 24
    "Don't Say Gay" legislation, 40
    See also LGBTQIA+ community
gender
    of ALA members, 88
    definition of, 20
    equality, 16
    norms, 23, 32
gender confirmation surgery (GCS)
    description of, 77
    insurance coverage of, 72
    for transgender people, 81
    for transition, 76
gender dysphoria, 72
gender expression
    conversion therapy, 72–73
    definition of, 26
    overview of, 22–23
    transition, 76–77
gender identity
    bias, 25
    conversion therapy, 72–73
    definition of, 26
    gender expression vs., 22
    gender inclusivity at public library, 21–22
    librarian understanding of, 20
    overview of, 20–21

trans students, protection of, 75
transition, 76–77
GenderWatch database (ProQuest), 119
Georgia, 7
Getting It: A Guide to Hot, Healthy Hookups and Shame-Free Sex (Moon), 118
GLAAD (Gay & Lesbian Alliance Against Defamation), 117, 118
GLMA (Health Professionals Advancing LGBTQ Equality), 80, 118
"The Global Health Database for the Public Health Digital Library" (Global Health), 119
Go Aunt Flow, 104
gonorrhea, 38
Google News alert, 96
Griswold v. Connecticut, 34
Gunter, Jen, 114
Gurr, Barbara Anne, 116
Gutiérrez, Elena R., 116
Guttmacher Institute
  on access to SRH information, 16
  online resources of, 115
  "Sex and HIV Education," 40
  on sexual and reproductive health, 4
  state abortion law information, 60
  on sterilization services, 35
gynecologic cancers, 65, 100
gynecological exams, 74

H

Happy Scribe, 94
Hardwick, Michael, 75
Hathcock, April, 114
health
  See sexual health
Health and Medical Reference Guidelines (RUSA), 91
health care
  CDC's STI Treatment Guidelines Timeline, 37
  court cases/legislation on LGBTQIA+ health care, 74–75
  health literacy and, 91–92
  LGBTQIA+ community and, 71–74
  library and, 99
  for pregnant transgender people, 78
  sexuality and, 25–26
health insurance
  LGBTQIA+ people and, 74
  menstrual products and, 103
health literacy
  resources for continuing education, 106
  SRH information integration into library, 91–92
Health Professionals Advancing LGBTQ Equality (GLMA), 80, 118
Healthy People 2030 (microsite), 115
Helping Public Libraries Meet Community Health Needs (NNLM), 106
hepatitis B, 38
herpes simplex virus (HSV), 38
heterosexual, 24
Hill, Maisie, 115
Hispanic Americans, 88
HIV (human immunodeficiency virus), 38–39
Hodges, Obergefell v., 75
homelessness, 74
hormonal birth control
  contraception for LGBTQIA+ community, 80
  for endometriosis treatment, 53–54
  most popular types of birth control, 34
hormone therapy (HT)
  description of, 76–77
  in medical transition, 76
  review of, 81
hospitals, 98
How's It Hanging? Expert Answers to the Questions Men Don't Always Ask (Baum & Miller), 114
HSV (herpes simplex virus), 38
Hughes, Kathleen, 114
human immunodeficiency virus (HIV), 38–39
human papillomavirus (HPV), 38
human rights
  abortion as human right, 61
  menstruation as human rights issue, 52–53
  sexual health depends on, 32
  SRH information access as, 15–16
Human Rights Campaign, 39, 118
Hyde Amendment, 6
hysterectomies, 54
hysterectomy
  description of, 54
  for gender confirmation surgery, 77
  for sterilization of women, 7

Index

I

Ibis Reproductive Health, 115
idea file, 95, 111
identity
    See gender identity
identity work
    importance of, 106
    library anxiety and, 87–89
In on It: What Adoptive Parents Would Like You to Know about Adoption: A Guide for Relatives and Friends (O'Toole), 115
In Our Own Voice: National Black Women's Reproductive Justice Agenda, 8
In Their Voices: Black Americans on Transracial Adoption. (Roorda), 115
in vitro fertilization (IVF), 57, 78
inclusivity
    gender inclusivity at public library, 21–22
    importance of, xi
Indian Health Service Plan, 6
indigenous people, 6–7
Indigenous Women Rising, 116
infant formula, 63
infertility, 57
information access, 49–50
Information Services to Diverse Populations: Developing Culturally Competent Library Professionals (Cooke), 89, 113
intellectual freedom, 13–14
interACT: Advocates for Intersex Youth, 73, 118
International Conference on Population and Development, Cairo, 1994, 6–9
International Journal of Transgender Health, 119
intersectionality
    definition of, 25
    in library, 26
    library collections and, 27
intersex individuals, 73
intimate partner violence (IPV), 42
intracytoplasmic sperm injection (ICSI), 57
intrauterine devices (IUDs), 34
intrauterine insemination (IUI), 57

J

Johns Hopkins, 53
Johnson, Margaret E., 103
Journal of Adolescent Health, 61
Journal of Pain Research, 50–51

K

Kaiser Family Foundation, 74, 115
"KFF—Health Policy Analysis, Polling, Journalism and Social Impact Media" (Kaiser Family Foundation), 115
Killing the Black Body: Race, Reproduction, and the Meaning of Liberty (Roberts), 116
Kirichanskaya, Michele, 72
"Know Your Rights: LGBTQ Rights" (ACLU), 117
"Knowledge Is Power: Serving Gender Diverse Youth in the Library" (Hughes), 114

L

Lancet Public Health, 32, 33
Langford, Jo, 117
LARC (long-acting reversible contraception), 34
Lavender Magazine, 118
Lawrence v. Texas, 75
legal landscape
    librarian understanding of, 110
    reference services on SRH and, 90
legislation
    about sex education in schools, 40
    on LGBTQIA+ sexual and reproductive health, 74–75
Lesbian, Gay, Bisexual, and Transgender Healthcare: A Clinical Guide to Preventive, Primary, and Specialist Care (Eckstrand & Ehrenfeld), 117
lesbians
    health care system and, 74
    risk of teen pregnancy, 79
    See also LGBTQIA+ community
"LGBT[Q] Youth Resources" (CDC), 117
"LGBTQ Resource List" (GLAAD), 117
LGBTQ: The Survival Guide for Lesbian, Gay, Bisexual, Transgender, and Questioning Teens (Madrone), 117
LGBTQ+ Source (EBSCO), 119
LGBTQAI+ Books for Children and Teens: Providing a Window for All (Dorr, Deskins, & Naidoo), 113
LGBTQIA+ community
    bias in health care, 25
    HIV among members of, 39
    PFLAG for, 19
    reproductive justice for, 8
    resources on LGBTQIA+ sexuality/health, 117–118

Index

sexual orientation, types of, 23–24
sexual violence experienced by, 41
SRH information for, 81
states with LGBTQIA+ curriculum ban, 40
support of, 80
LGBTQIA+ sexual and reproductive health topics
   contraception, 79–80
   court cases/legislation, 74–75
   final thoughts about, 81
   health care and LGBTQIA+ community, 71–74
   pregnancy, 77–78
   reflection questions about, 81
   review of, 81
   supporting LGBTQIA+ community, 80
   transition, 76–77
LibGuides, 92, 93
librarians
   collection development, SRH, 95–98
   content creation for patrons, 92–93
   gender inclusivity at public library, 21–22
   health literacy of patrons and, 91–92
   library anxiety/bias in public library services, 87–89
   moving forward with SRH, 109–112
   reproductive health information, 66
   reproductive justice and, 9
   sexual health resources for patrons, 31
   sexuality concepts and, 20
   SRH, demystifying, x
   SRH information access as core to, 13–15
   SRH information access as human right, 15–16
   SRH information access, personal beliefs and, 14
   SRH integration into library, 107
   SRH integration into reference services, 89–91
   SRH programs/community collaborations, 98–102
   stories about patrons reference questions, ix–x
   support of LGBTQIA+ community, 80
   See also reflection questions
libraries
   contraception/pregnancy prevention information at, 79–80
   gender inclusivity at public library, 21–22
   implementation of SRH information, 85
   menstrual justice at, 103–105
   moving forward with SRH, 109–112
   sexual harassment in, 43
   sexual harassment in library, 43
   sexual violence prevention information, 42
   SRH information access as core to, 13–15
   SRH information access as human right, 15–16
   SRH information access via, 17, 26
   SRH integration into reference services, 89–91
   STI stigma, reduction of, 39
   support of LGBTQIA+ community, 80, 81
library, SRH information integration
   anxiety/bias in public library services, 87–89
   collection development, 95–98
   content creation, 92–93
   continuing education resources, 106
   final thoughts about, 106
   health literacy, 91–92
   menstrual justice at library, 103–105
   programs/community collaborations, 98–99, 102
   reference services, 89–91
   reflection questions, 107
   review of, 107
   SRH program/partnership ideas, 100–102
   SRH resource guide ideas, 93
   tutorials, 94–95
library anxiety
   definition of, 87
   identity work and, 87–89
"Library Anxiety: A Grounded Theory and Its Development" (Mellon), 114
Library Bill of Rights (American Library Association)
   SRH information access and, 17
   on upholding intellectual freedom, 13–14
library patrons
   See patrons
library service, SRH information as
   final thoughts about, 16
   reflection questions about, 17

Index

library service, SRH information as (cont'd)
  review of, 17
  SRH information access as core to libraries, 13–15
  SRH information access as human right, 15–16
library-related resources, organizations, articles, 113–114
literacy, health, 91–92
Liu, Vic, 118
local groups, 99
long-acting reversible contraception (LARC), 34
Love Worth Making: How to Have Ridiculously Great Sex in a Long-Lasting Relationship (Snyder), 119
Luna, Zakiya, 116

M

Madrone, Kelly Huegel, 117
magazines, 118
Maglaty, Jeanne, 23
Maltz, Wendy, 118
mammogram, 62–63
The Managed Body (Bobel), 104
marginalized communities, 6–9
marital rape, 41–42
marriage, same-sex, 75
Marty, Robin, 115
Mayo Clinic
  on adenomyosis, 54
  on infertility, 57
  on risk reduction for STIs, 38
Mayo Clinic Guide to a Healthy Pregnancy (Wick), 115
Me Too movement, 41
medical abortion, 60
medical transition, 76
MedlinePlus, 98
Mellon, Constance A., 87, 114
men
  breast cancer in, 62
  gender norms through time, 23
  prostate cancer and, 64
  sterilization of, 35
  testicular/penile cancer, 64–65
menarche, 50
menopause, 52
The Menopause Manifesto: Own Your Health with Facts and Feminism (Gunter), 114
menstrual injustice, 103

menstrual justice
  at library, 103–105
  library advancement of, 107
  menstruation as human rights issue, 52–53
menstrual pain (dysmenorrhea), 50–51
menstrual products
  menstrual justice, 52–53
  menstrual product drive, 105
  tampon tax, 103
MenstrualHygieneDay.org, 107
menstruation
  as human rights issue, 52–53
  menstrual interruptions/absence, 51–52
  menstrual justice at library, 103–105
  overview of, 50–51
  as part of reproductive health care, 66
  perimenopause/menopause, 52
  uterine fibroids and, 54
mental illness, 71–72
Mexican Americans, 7
Milken Institute, 91
Miller, Scott, 114
Mintz, Laurie B., 118
miscarriage
  description of, 58–59
  SRH resource guide ideas, 93
Moon, Allison, 118
Movement Advancement Project (MAP), 40, 118
"Multicultural Education Pavilion—Diversity, Equity, and Social Justice Education Resources" (web page), 114

N

Nagoski, Emily, 118
Naidoo, Jamie Campbell, 113
National Coalition for LGBTQ Health, 118
National Council of Negro Women, 34
National LGBTQ Task Force, 118
National LGBTQIA+ Health Education Center, 118
National Women's Law Center, 117
national/international observances, 100–102
Native Americans and Alaska Natives
  lack of diversity in libraries, 88
  pregnancy-related deaths among women, 8
  reproductive justice for, lack of, 6–7

Native Hawaiians or Other Pacific Islanders, 88
needs assessment, community, 102
Network of the National Library of Medicine (NNLM), 106
New Handbook for a Post-Roe America: The Complete Guide to Abortion Legality, Access, and Practical Support (Marty), 115
New York StateWide Senior Action Council (StateWide), 99
news alerts, 111
Nienow, Mary C., 114
nonbinary people, 21
nonprocreative sex laws, 75
Nordell, Jessica, 114
norms
    gender expression and, 22
    gender norms, 20
North American Society for Pediatric and Adolescent Gynecology, 61
North Carolina, 7

O

Obama, Barack, 75
Obergefell v. Hodges, 75
Office on Women's Health (website), 116
Okamoto, Nadya, 104
older adults, 38
One Package, United States v., 34
online resources, 116–117
Open to All: Serving the GLBT Community in Your Library (toolkit) (ALA GLBTRT), 113
oral contraceptives, 34
organizational health literacy, 91
organizations
    abortion, support for, 60–61
    library-related resources, organizations, articles, 113–114
    list of potential SRH partners, 111
    partnerships with, 42, 74
    for sexuality/LGBTQIA health, 118
Oswego County Opportunities (OCO), 99
O'Toole, Elisabeth, 115
Our Bodies, Ourselves (Boston Women's Health Collective), 114
Out magazine, 118
ovarian cancer, 65
ovaries, 50, 52
ovulation, 50

P

Pad Project, 116
pain, 50–51
Pan American Health Organization (PAHO), 31
pansexual, 24
pap smear, 65
Parker, Lara, 115
partner-assisted reproduction, 78
partnerships
    for health literacy, 91–92
    list of potential SRH partners, 111
    SRH program/partnership ideas, 100–102
    SRH programs/community collaborations, 98–99, 102
pathologization, 71–72, 81
patrons
    content creation for, 92–93
    health literacy of, 91–92
    library anxiety/bias in public library services, 87–89
    library SRH services for, 111–112
    menstrual justice at library and, 104
    power dynamics between librarian and, 110
    reference questions about sex, ix–x
    sexual harassment in library, 43
    SRH information at library and, 107
    SRH integration into reference services, 89–91
PCOS (polycystic ovary syndrome), 51, 57
penicillin, 36
penile cancer, 64–65
The Penis Book: A Doctor's Complete Guide to the Penis—from Size to Function and Everything in Between (Spitz), 115
people of color, 5, 6–8
Peoples, Whitney, 116
perimenopause, 52
Perimenopause Power: Navigating Your Hormones on the Journey to Menopause (Hill), 115
period
    See menstruation
Period. End of Sentence (Diamant), 103, 104
period poverty, 53, 103–105
Period Power (Okamoto), 104
period tracking, 105
Periods Gone Public: Taking a Stand for Menstrual Equity (Weiss-Wolf), 104, 115

Index

personal health literacy, 91–92
Pessin-Whedbee, Brook, 117
PFLAG
  link for, 118
  "PFLAG National Glossary of Terms," 19, 117
pleasure
  consent and, 39
  sexual pleasure, 32, 33
  sexual pleasure and consent resources, 118–119
police brutality, 8
policies, library, 97
polycystic ovary syndrome (PCOS), 51, 57
"Poor Communities Exposed to Elevated Air Pollution Levels" (Failey), 35–36
population, 35–36
postpartum depression (PPD), 58
postpartum eclampsia, 56
postpartum psychosis, 58
post-traumatic stress disorder, 41
power dynamics, 110
preeclampsia, 56
pregnancy
  birthing options, 58
  complications, 55–56
  contraception for prevention of, 32–34
  Crisis Pregnancy Centers, 61–62
  fertility/infertility/pregnancy options, 56–57
  LGBTQIA+ people and, 77–78, 79
  miscarriage, 58–59
  overview of, 55
  pregnancy-related deaths, 8
  resources about, provision of, 66
  resources for LGBTQIA+ community, 81
  sterilization to prevent, 35–36
PRH Physicians for Reproductive Health, 116
The Pride Guide: A Guide to Sexual and Social Health for LGBTQ Youth (Langford), 117
prison industrial complex, 8
Programming Librarian website, 99
programs
  SRH information integration into library, 98–99, 102
  SRH program/partnership ideas, 100–102
promotion
  menstrual product drive, 105
  of resource guide, 94

pronouns
  gender inclusivity at public library, 21–22
  transition process and, 76
ProQuest, 119
prostate, 64
public health, 32, 33
public libraries
  gender inclusivity at, 21–22
  reproductive justice material, need for, 9
  SRH collection development, 95–98
  SRH information access as core to, 13–15
  SRH information mission, 4
  SRH information/services, 10
Public Library Association, 106
public schools, 40
PubMed, 119
Puerto Rico, 6–7

Q

QR code, 94, 98
queer, 24
  See also LGBTQIA+ community
Queer Sex: A Trans and Non-binary Guide to Intimacy, Pleasure and Relationships (Roche), 119
questioning, 24
questions
  See reflection questions

R

race/ethnicity
  lack of diversity in libraries, 88
  reproductive justice and, 6–8
Radical Reproductive Justice: Foundation, Theory, Practice, Critique (Ross, Roberts, Derkas, Peoples, Toure, & Roberts), 116
rape, 41–42
Rape, Abuse, and Incest National Network (RAINN), 41
reciprocal IVF, 78
Reference and User Services Association (RUSA), 90, 91
reference interview, 90
reference services
  library anxiety/bias in public library services, 87–89
  questions about sex/reproductive health, ix–x

Index

for SRH information, 107
SRH integration into, 89–91, 107
reflection questions
    as consideration opportunities, xii
    LGBTQIA+ SRH topics, 81
    reproductive health, 66
    sexual and reproductive health, 10
    sexual and reproductive health information as library service, 17
    sexual health, 44
    sexuality, 27
    SRH information, integration into library, 107
religious beliefs, 61
The Remedy: Queer and Trans Voices on Health and Health Care (Sharman), 117
Reproducing Empire: Race, Sex, Science, and U.S. Imperialism in Puerto Rico (Briggs), 116
Reproduction on the Reservation: Pregnancy, Childbirth, and Colonialism in the Long Twentieth Century (Theobald), 6
reproductive health
    abortion, 59–61
    adoption, 59
    birthing options, 58
    breast health, 62–63
    breastfeeding, 63–64
    cancers, 64–65
    crisis pregnancy centers, 61–62
    databases, 119
    definition of, 3–4
    endometriosis, uterine fibroids, adenomyosis, 53–54
    fertility, infertility, pregnancy options, 56–57
    final thoughts about, 65–66
    hysterectomies, 54
    menstrual interruptions/absence, 51–52
    menstruation, 50–51
    menstruation as human rights issue, 52–53
    overview of, 49–50
    perimenopause/menopause, 52
    pregnancy, 55–56
    pregnancy loss, 58–59
    prostate, 64
    reflection questions, 66
    resources on, 114–116
    review of, 66
"Reproductive Health" resource (CDC), 115
Reproductive Justice: An Introduction (Ross & Solinger), 116
reproductive justice (RJ)
    in American history, 6–9
    barriers to, 49
    coining of term, 5
    definition of, 6
    as holistic lens, 109
    population growth and, 36
    resources on, 116–117
    review of, 9–10
Reproductive Justice: The Politics of Health Care for Native American Women (Gurr), 116
Reproductive Rights as Human Rights: Women of Color and the Fight for Reproductive Justice (Luna), 116
research, 14
resource guide
    choosing your SRH tutorial topic, 95
    content creation for patrons, 92–93
    SRH resource guide ideas, 93
    tutorials, creating, 94
resources
    for continuing education on SRH, 106
    library-related resources, organizations, articles, 113–114
    reproductive and sexual health, 114–116
    reproductive justice, 116–117
    sexual and reproductive health databases, 119
    on sexual pleasure and consent, 118–119
    sexuality and LGBTQIA+ health, 117–118
rights
    sexual and reproductive health, 3, 4
    SRH information access as human right, 15–16
    See also human rights
RJ
    See reproductive justice
Roberts, Dorothy E., 116
Roberts, Lynn, 116
Roche, Juno, 119
Roe v. Wade
    overturning of, 60
    periods and, 105
    reversal of, 96
Roorda, Rhonda M., 115
Roosevelt, Franklin Delano, 23
Ross, Loretta
    Reproductive Justice: An Introduction, 116

Index

Ross, Loretta (cont'd)
 Undivided Rights: Women of Color Organizing for Reproductive Justice, 116
RUSA (Reference and User Services Association), 90, 91

S

same-sex marriage, 75
The Savvy Ally: A Guide for Becoming a Skilled LGBTQ+ Advocate (Gainsburg), 117
schools, sex education in, 40
Scopus, 119
SDGs (Sustainable Development Goals), 15–16
semen
 infertility, 57
 made by prostate, 64
 vasectomy and, 35
sex
 definition of, 20, 26
 gender identity and, 20–21
 intersex individuals, 73
sex education, 40
Sex Talk As Real Talk program, 100
Sex Up Your Life: The Mind-Blowing Path to True Intimacy, Healing, and Hope (Archambault), 118
sex&u.ca, 116
SexEd Library, 116
sexting, 41
sexual abuse, 41–42
"Sexual and Reproductive Health and Research (SRH)" (World Health Organization), 116
sexual and reproductive health at library
 anxiety/bias in public library services, 87–89
 collection development, 95–98
 content creation, 92–93
 continuing education resources, 106
 final thoughts about, 106
 health literacy, 91–92
 menstrual justice at library, 103–105
 programs/community collaborations, 98–99, 102
 reference services, 89–91
 reflection questions, 107
 review of, 107
 SRH program/partnership ideas, 100–102
 SRH resource guide ideas, 93
 tutorials, 94–95
sexual and reproductive health information as library service
 final thoughts about, 16
 reflection questions about, 17
 review of, 17
 SRH information access as core to libraries, 13–15
 SRH information access as human right, 15–16
sexual and reproductive health (SRH)
 databases, 119
 definition of, 3–4
 final thoughts about, 9
 librarian's moves for, 111–112
 meaning of, 31
 moving forward with, 109–112
 next steps for library, 111
 overview of book's coverage of, xi–xiii
 reference questions about, ix–x
 reflection questions, 10
 reproductive justice, 5–9
 resources on, 114–116
 review of chapter on, 9–10
 summary of coverage of, 109–111
 topics, 4–5
sexual and reproductive rights
 Guttmacher Institute on, 4
 WHO on, 3
sexual expression
 librarian understanding of, 20
 sexual health and, 32
sexual harassment, 43
The Sexual Healing Journey: A Guide for Survivors of Sexual Abuse (Maltz), 118
sexual health
 contraception, 32–34
 final thoughts about, 44
 four pillars of comprehensive public health approach to sexuality, 32, 33
 overview of, 31–32
 reflection questions, 44
 review of, 44
 sex education in schools, 40
 sexual harassment in library, 43
 sexual pleasure/consent, 39
 sexual violence, 41–42
 sexually transmitted infections, 36–39
 sterilization, 35–36
 WHO on, 3
sexual justice, 32, 33

Index

sexual orientation
    conversion therapy, 72–73
    definition of, 27
    librarian understanding of, 20
    overview of, 23–24
sexual pleasure
    definition of, 39
    four pillars of comprehensive public health approach to sexuality, 32, 33
    resources on, 118–119
sexual violence
    definition of, 41
    discourse/action regarding, 41–42
    prevention information, 42
    review of, 44
    sex education in schools about, 40
sexual well-being, 32, 33
sexuality
    final thoughts about, 26
    four pillars of comprehensive public health approach to sexuality, 32, 33
    gender expression, 22–23
    gender identity, 20–21
    gender inclusivity at public library, 21–22
    gender norms through time, 23
    health and, 25–26
    overview of, 19–20
    reflection questions, 27
    resources LGBTQIA+ sexuality/health, 117–118
    review of, 26–27
    sex/gender, 20
    sexual orientation, 23–24
sexually transmitted infections (STIs)
    CDC's STI Treatment Guidelines Timeline, 37
    overview of, 36–38
    review of, 44
    stigmatization of, 38–39
Sharman, Zena, 117
shelf talkers, 90
signage, 90
silence, 44
Silliman, Jael, 116
Sims, James Marion, 7–8
SisterSong Women of Color Reproductive Justice Collective, 5, 117
slavery, 7–8
SNAP (Supplemental Nutrition Assistance Program), 103

Snyder, Stephen, 119
social stigma, 81
social transition, 76
society, 22–23
Society of Adolescent Health and Medicine, 61
Society of Obstetricians and Gynaecologists of Canada, 116
Solinger, Rickie, 116
Sosin, Kate, 40
sperm
    donation, 57, 77–78
    in fertilization, 55
    freezing, 78
Spitz, Aaron, 115
SRH
    See sexual and reproductive health
states, sex education in schools, 40
stereotypes, 88–89
sterilization
    of Native American women, 6
    overpopulation argument for, 35–36
    overview of, 35
    of Puerto Rican women, 6–7
stigma
    of LGBTQIA+ community, 81
    library anxiety/bias in public library services, 88
    of periods, 104
    silence and, 44
    of STIs, 38–39
stillbirth, 58–59
STIs
    See sexually transmitted infections
STOP SV: A Technical Package to Prevent Sexual Violence (CDC), 42
subscription, 111
Supplemental Nutrition Assistance Program (SNAP), 103
support, of LGBTQIA+ community, 80
surgery
    See gender confirmation surgery
surgical abortion, 60
surrogacy, 57, 78
survivors, of sexual violence, 41–42
Sustainable Development Goals (SDGs), 15–16
syphilis, 38

T

"tampon tax," 103
Tando, Darlene, 117

Index

taxes, 103
teenagers, 79–80
telehealth appointments, 99
Tennessee, 7
terms, 19
testicular cancer, 64–65
Texas, Lawrence v., 75
Them magazine, 118
Theobald, Brianna, 6
Title IX, 75
Tough Topics sign, 90
Toure, Pamela Bridgewater, 116
Transgender Health: A Practitioner's Guide to Binary and Non-binary Trans Patient Care (Vincent), 117
transgender people
    barriers/social stigma of, 81
    characteristics of, 21
    contraception for, 79–80
    gender dysphoria term, 72
    health care system and, 74
    pregnancy options for, 77–78
    trans students, Title IX protection of, 75
    transition, 76–77
    See also LGBTQIA+ community
transition
    library resources about, 81
    overview of, 76–77
transsexual people, 76–77
Trevor Project, 118
trichomoniasis, 38
Trump, Donald, 8, 75
tubal ligations, 35
Turnaway Study, 61
The Turnaway Study: Ten Years, a Thousand Women, and the Consequences of Having—or Being Denied—an Abortion (Foster), 114
Turner syndrome, 51–52
tutorials, 94–95

U

Understanding Gynecological Cancer program, 100
Undivided Rights: Women of Color Organizing for Reproductive Justice (Silliman, Fried, Ross, & Gutiérrez), 116
United Nations
    on abortion, 61
    on menstruation as human rights issue, 53
    Sustainable Development Goals, 15–16
United Nations Population Fund, 3
United States
    contraception in, 33–34
    STIs in, 38
United States Preventive Services Task Force (USPSTF), 63
United States v. One Package, 34
Universal Declaration of Human Rights (UDHR), 15
University of California, Los Angeles (UCLA), 41
University of California–Davis, 42
University of Kansas, 102
updates, 96, 97
"The Urgency of Intersectionality" (Crenshaw), 26
U.S. Census Bureau, 88
US Circuit Court of Appeals, 34
U.S. Department of Education, 75
U.S. Department of Health and Human Services (HHS), 91, 115
U.S. Supreme Court
    Buck v. Bell, 7
    Griswold v. Connecticut, 34
    Obergefell v. Hodges, 75
    Roe v. Wade, 60, 96
USAID, 6–7
users
    See patrons
uterine cancer, 65
uterine fibroids, 54
uterus
    endometriosis, 53–54
    hysterectomies, 54
    pregnancy, 55

V

vaccination, 38
Vagina Problems: Endometriosis, Painful Sex, and Other Taboo Topics (Parker), 115
vaginal cancer, 65
vasectomy, 35
Vincent, Ben, 117
violence
    LGBTQIA+ community and, 25, 75
    sex education in schools about, 40
    sexual and reproductive rights, 4
    sexual health as free of, 3, 32, 39
    sexual violence, 41–42, 44
virtual meetings, 99

Index

"Vocational Awe and Librarianship: The Lies We Tell Ourselves" (Ettarh), 114
vulvar cancer, 65

W

Wade, Roe v.
  overturning of, 60
  periods and, 105
  reversal of, 96
wage gaps, 8
Walbert, David F., 115
WAS (World Association for Sexual Health), 31
Waukegan (IL) Public Library, 99
"We Could Do Better": Librarian Engagement in LGBTQ Collection Development in Small and Rural Public Libraries in the Southern U.S." (Betts-Green), 113
webinar, 111
website, library
  links to health resources from, 98
  tutorial on, 94
websites
  online reproductive and sexual health resources, 115–116
  online reproductive justice resources, 116–117
  online sexuality and LGBTQIA+ health resources, 117–118
  resources for continuing education, 106
  sexual and reproductive health databases, 119
weeding, 96, 107
Weiss-Wolf, Jennifer, 104, 115
welcoming environment, 110
well-being
  in reproductive health definition, 49
  sexual well-being, 32, 33
West Virginia, 7
"When Did Girls Start Wearing Pink?" (Maglaty), 23
White Americans
  lack of diversity in libraries, 88
  quality of health care for, 15
  reproductive justice and, 7
"White Librarianship in Blackface: Diversity Initiatives in LIS" (Hathcock), 114
Who Are You? The Kid's Guide to Gender Identity (Pessin-Whedbee & Bardoff), 117

Whole Person Librarianship: A Social Work Approach to Patron Services (Zettervall & Nienow), 114
Whose Choice Is It? Abortion, Medicine, and the Law (Walbert & Butler), 115
WIC (Women, Infants, and Children), 103
Wick, Myra J., 115
women
  abortion and, 59–61
  breast health, 62–63
  breastfeeding by, 63–64
  disparities in quality of health care for, 14
  endometriosis, uterine fibroids, adenomyosis, 53–54
  gender bias in health care, 25
  gender equality goal of SDG, 16
  LGBTQIA+, health care system and, 74
  menstrual justice at library, 103–105
  menstruation, 50–52
  menstruation as human rights issue, 52–53
  perimenopause/menopause, 52
  reproductive justice and, 5–9
  sterilization of, 35
  See also pregnancy; reproductive health
Women's Reproductive Health (journal), 104
World Association for Sexual Health (WAS), 31
World Health Organization (WHO)
  on abortion care, 16
  on breast milk, 63
  on health care information/gender, 25
  on infertility, 57
  on sexual and reproductive health, 3
  "Sexual and Reproductive Health and Research (SRH)," 116
  on sexual health conceptual elements, 31–32
  on sexual health information, 15
  on STIs, 36
World Professional Association for Transgender Health (WPATH)
  contraception search directory, 80
  link for, 118
  standards-of-care document for medical transition, 76

Y

Your Pregnancy and Childbirth: Month to Month (American College of Obstetricians and Gynecologists), 115

Index

youth
    conversion therapy among, 72–73
    LGBTQIA+ youth, 79–80
    See also children
YouTube, 94

Z

Zerrenner, Emily, 103–105
Zettervall, Sara K., 114